Linda
A Full, Happy Life

RUDY SCHOUTEN

Braughler™
Books
braughlerbooks.com

The views and opinions expressed in this work are those of the author and do not necessarily reflect the views and opinions of Braughler Books LLC.

Photo restoration and enhancements by Ron Schouten

Printed in the United States of America
Published by Braughler Books LLC., Springboro, Ohio

First printing, 2022

ISBN: 978-1-955791-23-6

Library of Congress Control Number: 2021921922

Ordering information: Special discounts are available on quantity purchases by bookstores, corporations, associations, and others. For details, contact the publisher at:

sales@braughlerbooks.com

or at 937-58-BOOKS

For questions or comments about this book, please write to:

info@braughlerbooks.com

Braughler™ Books
braughlerbooks.com

*To Austin and Lucille Bradley
and their children: Tom, Greg, Cindy, and Steve*

*They gave Linda Bradley a good family
…and a happy life*

Contents

Contents

Introduction

Linda Darlene Bradley loved to tell a story, sometimes a little loudly because her excitement was way too big for a softer version. She was grateful for an audience, but she wasn't one to go on and on just to hear herself talk. She really wanted you to understand her, and she was happy, almost relieved, when you did.

She could listen, too, but it wasn't the kind of listening you demonstrate by raising an eyebrow or nodding your head; it was the kind that might come with a blank expression because you're so focused on letting the wheels turn. And more often than not, when she was finished thinking, the first thing out of her mouth was sharp and funny and brutally honest. It told you she understood the world a lot more clearly than you thought she did.

Those were qualities about Linda that took a minute to unpack. Most everything else emerged in a small explosion —the crop of bright red hair, the incandescent smile, and the soft arms ready to open wide and without inhibition for the next available hug. She didn't know a stranger, and I was a stranger she didn't know in 1975 when I took her sister out for the first time. Three years later, I was lucky enough to have Linda for a sister-in-law.

None of that qualifies me, particularly, for writing a book about her. Only her family knows—can *really* know—her story from the inside out. Only they can see and feel and understand completely what it was to be her parent, her brother, or her sister from day one in a lifelong experience common to them alone. And while the same might be said for any member of any family, it has always felt particularly true of Linda, who bore a special presence by virtue of her bold personality and a certain, natural confidence in overcoming the challenges in her life.

Those closest to her have, nonetheless, eagerly shared their memories of her to round out the ones I gathered over the years. What is most unique about Linda as the subject of a book is her triumph over a disability, but she is not a story without the family through which she flourished. Linda was born a colorful character with a condition hell-bent on defining her. Those things draw extra attention, some good and some not so good. She needed special help now and then. It could get complicated. But she was never more and never less a member of the family than any of the other Bradleys. And that's why she succeeded, and why she is so noteworthy.

The work of writing this book came with a couple of natural dilemmas, the first of which is the flip side of being in on all those memories: So many others, no doubt, have been lost or forgotten over time. There are wonderful anecdotes about Linda that could not find their way into these pages. But if this account of her life can help draw a few of them out among those who knew and loved her, that alone would be a happy outcome.

Another puzzle has to do with wondering what in the world Linda's parents would have thought about seeing Linda's story in print. They were private people, and it isn't hard to imagine them saying they wouldn't want anyone making a fuss over Linda or their work in helping her become who she was. But if they did, how would they have wanted the story told? It's one open to a certain amount of interpretation, so I can't deny some apprehension over the possibility I might have missed the mark on some of it. I can only hope they would forgive me for anything in here that they would have written a little differently.

This version of her story begins with the origins of the Bradley family, the footprints left by two very good people who would make plenty of room in their lives for Linda. It traces her progress through the trial and error of early programs for kids with Down syndrome. It peeks into what school and work and social life looked like for her, and what Mom and Dad did to uncover and navigate the kind of opportunities only beginning to unfold in the '50s and '60s.

But the heart of the book is the big personality in Linda—the wit, the fire, the innocence, the compassion, and the pure love in her—all of it so evident in the little stories retold affectionately by the most ardent members of her enormous fan club, her extended family. She left an indelible mark, the kind that tends to wash over the normal melancholy in a person's life to leave only very happy memories.

PART ONE

Life Before Linda
The Bradley Family: Beginnings

Lucille Nolan and Austin Bradley grew up in Indiana's version of the Deep South, where they soaked up youth and family life on farmland bordering the Hoosier National Forest.

Those who knew them well would marvel at the speed of life; the Nolan-Bradley chapter of the family ancestry is already more than a hundred years old. Lucille was born in July 1918 in Loogootee (pronounced, *la-goat-tea*), which sits just inside the western edge of Martin County. She and her older brother, Roy, and her younger sister, Rita, were the children of Martin Nolan and Margaret (Mullin) Nolan, and like most of the neighbors in this farming community, Martin and Maggie and their young threesome enjoyed simple country living, which is not to be confused with *easy* living. They grew into family life sharecropping a plot of land along Route 550 and lived in rental property known as the Houghton House—a well-worn but stately landmark dating back to the area's early settlers.

Austin was born a year later, in May 1919, on the Bradley family farm in Montgomery, which is in neighboring Daviess County. As the handy second oldest among the boys, he emerged quickly as a natural when it came to helping his father, Frank Bradley, and his mother, Irene (Williams) Bradley, with the chores. But he had plenty of help in the form of six hearty siblings—Bob, Betty, Louis, Margaret, Francis, and Patrick.

While Austin enjoyed the benefits of spending all of his child-hood at the same rural address, Lucille's family relocated at least once, but not by much. She hadn't yet reached her teens when Mom and Dad packed their things and headed west a mile or two, where they bought land and a farm all their own. The change of scenery was just enough to land her in the Daviess County school system, the one also tasked with educating the Bradley kids. So when Lucille enrolled as a sophomore at Barr Township High School in Montgomery, Austin was starting there as a freshman.

By all accounts, and likely by virtue of his work ethic, Austin sailed through high school without any major setbacks or shenan-igans, or at least none he thought worth mentioning. Lucille held her own in the classroom, too, despite a few complications in life outside the halls of learning. She was sick for the better part of a year, and her parents faced some rough patches in the uphill climb to carve out a living on the farm. It meant she'd have to miss some school not just to get well, but to do what she could to help them make the ends meet—a family decision not at all unusual for her day and age.

When Lucille reached her senior year, she took on part-time work in the evenings, away from the farm. It was the only way she could continue pitching in at home without dropping out of school. But by that point, she had missed enough time in the classroom to be a year behind, which meant that Austin Bradley, progressing along on schedule at Barr Township, caught up with Lucille for their final year; they graduated together in late April 1937.

It would have been fairly impossible for two people to attend the same school in Montgomery, Indiana, and not know one another, whether they were in the same class or not. In those days, Austin and Lucille crossed paths in the busy hallways and, in all likelihood, on the dance floor on a Friday night, but they didn't know each other *well*. And so it followed that after graduation, the two of them went their separate ways to take care of the business presenting itself at home.

In the larger scheme of things, life went on as it always did in Loogootee and Montgomery. In the summer following graduation, Austin took his first job outside the farming business when he went to work for Daviess County, setting utility poles that would carry the first electricity to the area's farming community. Lucille expanded her part-time job into full-time work at the Loogootee Pearl Button Works on Brickyard Road. The old factory thrived in the pre-synthetic, pre-zipper days of the clothing fastener industry by making buttons from the rich harvest of mussel shells in the nearby White River.

Austin continued to live at home in Montgomery for another couple of years before hearing the call from the big city. In 1939 he headed north 115 miles to the east side of Indianapolis and rented a house on Oxford Street. Within a few months he landed a job with Allison Division GMC as a machinist apprentice operating drill presses and milling machines. He advanced quickly within the ranks, taking advantage of as many company training opportunities as possible, including an eight-week course on blueprinting.

But Austin's upstart manufacturing career was about to get placed on hold. A notice of induction from the United States Selective Service arrived in his mailbox on December 4, 1941—three days before the Japanese attack on Pearl Harbor. Six months later, Austin entered active military service with the US Army and was assigned to two months of basic training at Selfridge Field in Michigan. But Uncle Sam and his wise minions saw enough in Austin to hold onto him beyond basic training for an additional

Lucille Nolan

Austin Bradley

five months of advanced technical school. Then they sent him overseas to a depot repair squadron in the Asiatic Pacific, where his assignments as a technician fifth grade included repairing airplane engines and climbing behind the controls of military cranes and cargo trucks.

Back home in Indiana, Lucille Nolan's post-high school adventures included seven more years of life on the farm and continued employment at the button factory. But in 1944, she too flew the coop and moved to Indianapolis to join the national cause; she took a job at the P.R. Mallory factory on East Washington Street, where she helped build the mercury batteries that powered portable electronic equipment used late in the war effort.

In some ways, those days went on, rather miraculously, as if nothing had changed. But it was a busy, perilous time; American men and women applying themselves diligently to a common, urgent purpose. Only some faced the horror of war directly, but everyone sacrificed something. And in the end, their kids, the children of the Greatest Generation, had no way of knowing just how long and dark and difficult those days may have been—because their parents, the ones who saw the darkest of it, tried so hard not to talk about it.

Corporal Austin Bradley served his country with distinction for three-and-a-half years and was honorably discharged from the Army in late December 1945. When he returned to his old job at Allison's, he was greeted with a layoff, the reward for his trouble. But he was an eminently reasonable man and understood the circumstances. He was just one of thousands coming home to jobs that had gone away—projects suspended and factory positions now occupied by someone else. He was also not without skills, including the ones he had learned in the service. So in early 1946, Austin procured a public passenger chauffeur's license and began driving another kind of heavy conveyance: a Greyhound bus. He was just happy to be home and happy to have work.

In the meantime, like so many other members of the Barr Township class of '37, Austin Bradley and Lucille Nolan had lost track of one another, largely by doing nothing to keep it. The war and the years would have been enough to separate good friends, let alone casual acquaintances. So, by the spring of 1946, Austin and Lucille had settled, separately and unaware of one another, into gainful post-war employment in the same new city and apartments on the same side of town. And just as it's supposed to happen in a small world, connections would conspire to reacquaint them.

Nina Everly grew up in Petersburg, Indiana, and like Lucille, moved north to Indy from rural southwest Indiana in the early 1940s to go to work at Mallory. The two strangers bumped into each other inside the plant one day, found a connection on the basis of their jobs on the line, and then discovered enough about each other on the personal side of life to become fast friends—on the job and then away from it.

And then there was Ralph Bradley. He wasn't actually related to Austin Bradley, but the two had been buddies back home in Montgomery, growing up on family farms not far apart. Like Austin, Ralph was cordially invited to join the nation's war efforts and served admirably before settling down to civilian life in Indianapolis. Each apparently preferred work in the transportation industry. While Austin drove for the bus company, Ralph took a job with the Penn Central Railroad. In the years since their days on the farm, they had gone off in separate directions, but Austin and Ralph would not lose track of one another. The friendship wouldn't allow it.

In any event, when Nina landed in Indy, she wasn't looking for anything beyond a good job and a fresh start. But a night out on the city's east side with a group of her new friends tagging along changed all that. Whether it was planned in advance or truly a chance meeting, Lucille Nolan introduced her to Ralph Bradley, who was, ironically, Lucille's distant cousin. Another connection was made; Ralph and Nina began making the rounds together, sometimes without the rest of the gang, and in relatively short order, they agreed on a date for a wedding, the spring of 1946, and a place to have it, St. Phillip Neri Catholic Church in Indianapolis.

Additional planning called for choosing friends to stand up for them at the service. Nina decided on Lucille Nolan, her new best friend from work and, now, apparent matchmaker; Ralph picked his old hometown buddy, Austin Bradley. Two old classmates at Barr Township High School in Montgomery were about to be reunited.

By all accounts, it was a fine wedding. Ralph and Nina Bradley got off to a great start on a long, happy marriage while Austin and Lucille were properly re-introduced, although without much fanfare. In the days leading up to the nuptials, and at the wedding itself, it hadn't occurred to either of them to make too much of the re-acquaintance, but they ended up enjoying the chance to spend a little time together. And as the wedding reception was breaking up, Austin found himself asking Lucille for her phone number. She gave it to him, as history would tell it, but not without first gaining some leverage in the infancy of their relationship. "I bet you never call me."

Lucille knew *something* about Austin Bradley, or maybe just something about human nature. Austin, on the other hand, didn't mind proving Lucille wrong, so he called her soon after the wedding to ask for an official date, and when that went well, they, too, began seeing each other on a regular basis. It was the beginning of a very good time in their lives—an era that included an active social life centered on date nights, family get-togethers bridging back to their days on the farm before the war, and the simple fun and freedom of running around with other young couples—the likes of Ralph and Nina Bradley, Paul and Peony Canfield, and May and Hank Schlemer.

Work life was agreeable, too. Lucille continued to prosper in her position at Mallory and Austin was happy with his work at the bus company; happy enough that he declined offers to return to his old job at Allison Division ... twice. He knew that his work as a machinist offered him the possibility of a brighter future, but didn't fully trust that it wouldn't go away again. He also, however, understood that he'd eventually have to take a chance on it. So in early 1947, Austin accepted what he knew might be a final overture and went back to work at Allison's. He never had to change jobs again.

Mr. and Mrs. Austin Bradley

The Ralph and Nina union that triggered the reconnection between Austin Bradley and Lucille Nolan led to another good wedding just a year later. On May 3, 1947, Austin and Lucille exchanged vows inside St. Martin Catholic Church, Lucille's parish back home in Loogootee. And very much in keeping with strong family connections, Austin's brother Louis and Lucille's sister Rita served as witnesses.

The newlyweds considered a few options in finding their first home together, including the possibility of moving back down south to Montgomery and the Bradley family farm. While three of Austin's brothers had joined him in his military service to Uncle Sam, a fourth brother, Francis, had been entrusted with the work of managing the family homestead while they were away. After the war, Austin, who still had some farming in his blood, made a point of checking in with Francis from time to time to make sure he wasn't ready to give it up. But Francis and his wife-to-be

Patty seemed very happy with the notion of country life, so Austin found it prudent to leave well enough alone—especially since Lucille hinted that she'd had enough of country life.

In the end, though, having good jobs in Indianapolis made fast work of their big decision, and the young couple opted for a rental in an old brick apartment building on Massachusetts Avenue, a spot downtown providing Lucille with an easy commute. It was a practical choice, but being downtown also offered them the benefit of being close to their friends and some of the better social life in the city. It suited them perfectly for a while, but they were also inclined to look to the future, and they could see the need for a place with room to grow in a more family-friendly setting. So in late 1948, Austin and Lucille left apartment life behind to rent a bungalow at 1506 East Tabor Street on the near northeast side, easily in time for the arrival of their firstborn, Tom, in February 1949.

Austin and Lucille enjoyed having their piece of the American dream and went about wrapping themselves around the new role of Mom and Dad. Tom liked the idea of having his parents, a bunch of toys, and the kids' room all to himself. But Mom and Dad eventually began to feel like what he really needed was a brother or a sister. So on October 8, 1951, they found themselves in the delivery room at Methodist Hospital in Indianapolis to usher Linda Darlene Bradley into the world.

PART TWO

The Doctor's Report
A Diagnosis: 1951

Lucille Bradley's doctor never suggested prenatal screenings or diagnostics to check on the baby. That would have been unusual in the absence of some indication of a problem. So, like other young women starting families in the early 1950s, Lucille just did what she knew to do. She ate well. She tried to get plenty of rest. And then, when the time came, she joined her husband in hoping and praying for the best. And their hopes and prayers were the normal kind for expectant moms and dads—filled with faith and cautious optimism, but not fear, because there was nothing to tell them there was anything to be afraid of.

That's why they froze in their tracks when the doctor delivered the news: Linda was born with Down syndrome.

Austin and Lucille probably reacted like other parents who had been where they were now. They may have stared at the messenger for a moment, and then somewhere off into space. A wave of *something* would have poured over them—something big enough to interrupt normal connections to the rest of the world. Things would have to sink in, just as they would have to sink in again later, and again after that. But in that moment, standing there with the doctor, they had no list of questions to ask because whatever it was they were thinking had to hang over them until the first question could find a way out.

When they finally rose to the surface, the questions that came to Austin and Lucille Bradley were less about what Down syndrome was than what it would mean. But they didn't get much help in either regard. The science available to define Linda's condition was limited. There were no social workers on hand to let them know what to expect; there were no support groups standing by to point them in the direction of the help they'd need.

The Bradleys had no way of knowing it yet, but in 1951, having a newborn with Down syndrome meant they would be on their own for the most part. It meant they would have to work very hard and be very patient to get Linda what she needed. And in the event they weren't willing or able to do those things, history would suggest that Linda Bradley had arrived in this world just a little too soon.

- It would be another ten years until President John F. Kennedy established the National Institute of Child Health and Human Development, which "conducted and supported research on mental retardation and all aspects of maternal and child health and human development."

- It would be another twelve years until the Mongoloid Development Council of Illinois would become the first known support group for families of children with Down syndrome in the United States.

- It would be another twenty years until the Education Act was passed, the first law in the United States to entitle children with disabilities to at least some education.

- It would be another thirty years until William I. Cohen's "Down Syndrome Preventative Medical Checklist" presented US doctors with their first medical management suggestions for treating people with Down syndrome.

- It would be another thirty-nine years until President George H. W. Bush signed the Americans with Disabilities Act, providing, for the first time, comprehensive civil rights protection for people with disabilities.

- It would be another forty-four years until the Disability Discrimination Act entitled children with Down syndrome to attend their local mainstream school.

- It would be another forty-six years until Patricia C. Winders published the first book on gross motor skills in children born with Down syndrome, presenting evidence-based therapies that could mean the difference between healthy walking and playing versus a lifetime of painful, debilitating hip and knee problems.

- And it would be fifty years until the American Academy of Pediatrics created "Health Supervision for Children with Down syndrome," guidelines for helping pediatricians and the parents of infants with Down syndrome—people like Austin and Lucille Bradley—learn how best to care for their children.

But the doctor who delivered Linda Bradley at Methodist Hospital that day couldn't very well look into the future. So when he sat down with Linda's parents to explain what Down syndrome was and to offer his best advice on what they should do, he was guided by a quick history of the syndrome and his grasp of the reality that surrounded him in 1951.

The National Down Syndrome Society tells us that we have probably always had people with Down syndrome among our numbers. "It wasn't until the late nineteenth century, however, that John Langdon Down, an English physician, published an accurate description of a person with Down syndrome. It was this scholarly work, published in 1866, that earned Down the recognition as the 'father' of the syndrome. Although other people had previously recognized the characteristics of the syndrome, it was Down who described the condition as a distinct and separate entity." Down linked this population to decreased intellectual ability and referred to them as "mongoloid" because he found their facial features to be similar to those of people native to Mongolia.

Some version of that history of Downs, enhanced by an overview of its common manifestations, may have been all the doctor could say to Austin and Lucille about the medical nature of their daughter's condition. But the focus of the conversation would not have been the diagnosis at all, but the advice he would give them. That was the bottom line, and as a result of his years of experience and the prevailing wisdom within his profession, it was also the part he was most sure of.

- In 1946, just five years before Linda's birth, the renowned pediatrician Benjamin Spock suggested that babies born "mongoloid" should be institutionalized. "If [the infant] merely exists at a level that is hardly human, it is much better for the other children and the parents to have him cared for elsewhere."

- Half of all Down syndrome babies suffered from heart defects. Other frequently co-occurring conditions included thyroid disease, obstructive sleep apnea, and leukemia. Medical procedures, sometimes relatively simple ones, could have saved or significantly prolonged their lives, but in 1951 most doctors refused to perform those services for people of any age with Down syndrome.

- It's the way it was—and pretty much the way it was three decades later when the Bloomington, Indiana, parents of

"Baby Doe" were advised by doctors to decline surgery to unblock their newborn's esophagus (a correctable condition)—because the baby had Down syndrome. The parents agreed to do nothing, and the baby starved to death before legal proceedings could compel the procedure.

- In 1951 and for many years before and after that, doctors and fathers conspired to tell mothers of newborns with Down syndrome that their babies had died, when, in reality, they had been quietly whisked away to inhumane institutions. The American playwright Arthur Miller fathered a son, Daniel, in the 1960s. The boy had Down syndrome, so Miller committed him to an institution and declined to visit with him or publicly acknowledge his existence for nearly forty years. It wasn't unusual.

The early 1950s were only the beginning of the end of two centuries of institutionalizing hundreds of thousands of developmentally disabled adults and children. That's what people did, and that's what the man who delivered Linda thought was right. So it wasn't surprising that his advice to her parents came with so much surety: "Linda will never master the basic skills she will need to become a productive member of society. She'll never be able to read or write. She'll never function normally, and even with a relatively healthy heart, she'll be lucky to survive into her twenties. Linda will be a drain on your family, and you should put her in an institution."

It took Austin and Lucille Bradley some time to come to terms with what Linda had, but there was never any question about what they would do. They said, simply, "Thank you, doctor, but we're taking Linda home with us."

PART THREE

A Lucky Landing
Linda's Childhood: 1951–1967

Coming Home

There was some business to take care of before Linda could leave the hospital. Mom and baby needed some time to get stronger and to show the medical people they were sufficiently fit for life on the outside. And Dad couldn't escape administrative matters and the usual paperwork for an official release.

But not all of the preparations were about medical care or hospital procedures. Austin and Lucille had listened carefully to what little the doctor could say about Linda's future, and they weren't taking any chances or wasting any time. They tracked down the Reverend James Higgins, Catholic chaplain at the hospital, and made arrangements to have their little girl baptized—just a little bit ahead of the usual time frame. Louis Bradley and Rita Nolan, the witnesses to Austin and Lucille's wedding four years earlier, came by to play another big role in their lives—to serve as Linda's godparents.

Cleared by the hospital and the good Lord, Linda was ready to go home. Mom and Dad were ready, too, but left Methodist Hospital without much in the way of instructions on the care of an infant with Down syndrome. It helped that they'd brought a baby home from the hospital once before—Tom was now 2½, but there was no reasonable way for them to understand the new challenges Linda might bring. They were nervous, of course,

Tom Bradley and baby sister

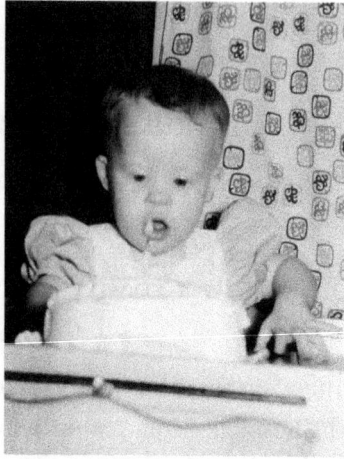
Linda's First Birthday

Mom enjoys her little girl

Tom all in on entertaining Linda

probably more than they let on, but trusted themselves to figure things out as they went along.

It was a wise approach because Linda proved, in every way other than the murky label that came with her, to be very much like any other little bundle. They loved her completely, and Linda wasted little time loving them right back with the kind of miracles that labeled her so much more justly: a wide-eyed sense of curiosity and a sweet, round face just barely wide enough to hold her big, happy grin.

Linda was a healthy, happy baby, and that's all Austin and Lucille really needed to see when they brought her home. But they knew that as the months went by, other more measurable attributes would begin to claim a share of their attention. Lucille, in particular, made a point of reading everything she could find about Downs to help her understand what to expect next. She tracked the little things Linda did—every new behavior and every detectable change in how she moved; all of it with an eye to what she had observed in older kids with Down syndrome and what she had read about them. But none of the manifestations of Linda's Down syndrome would be easy to figure out. Why would they be? Linda would be 8 years old by the time medical science discovered more precisely *what* it was.

The "Father of Down syndrome" had gotten the ball rolling with his research in 1866 documenting the characteristics of people with Downs, but it took another ninety-three years to determine the syndrome's specific origins. The National Down Syndrome Society has since summarized the discovery: "In 1959, the French physician Jérôme Lejeune identified Down syndrome as a chromosomal condition. Instead of the usual 46 chromosomes present in each cell, Lejeune observed 47 in the cells of individuals with Down syndrome. It was later determined that an extra partial or whole copy of chromosome 21 results in the characteristics associated with Down syndrome." Although there are two other types of Down syndrome (translocation and mosaicism), 95 percent of all cases are caused by this error in cell division known as "nondisjunction" or, more commonly, trisomy21.

The society's website goes on to lay a little more foundation under the definition. "In every cell in the human body there is a nucleus, where genetic material is stored in genes. Genes carry the codes responsible for all of our inherited traits and are grouped along rod-like structures called chromosomes. Typically, the nucleus of each cell contains 23 pairs of chromosomes, half of which are inherited from each parent. Down syndrome occurs when an individual has a full or partial extra copy of Chromosome 21. This additional genetic material alters the course of development and causes the characteristics associated with Down syndrome."

That's what Linda had: an extra chromosome.

And that's just one of the things Linda's parents could not know in 1951. What they *did* know included the usual boilerplate listing of physical characteristics associated with people who have Down syndrome—the "mongoloid" traits first identified by John Langdon Down and the more specific traits noted in the medical journals: "Eyes that have an upward slant, low muscle tone, small stature, short neck, flat nasal bridge, protruding tongue, and deep creases across the center of the palm."

They also knew that people born with Down syndrome have increased risk of heart defects, respiratory problems, hearing difficulties, epilepsy, and thyroid conditions. They tend to have "cognitive development profiles indicative of mild to moderate retardation, delayed speech and fine motor skills, and delays in meeting developmental milestones. The average age of sitting is 11 months, creeping is 17 months, and walking is 26 months."

Those were the things Lucille made a point to look for, maybe even expected to see, in Linda. But her monumental struggle to come to terms with all the challenges ahead for her daughter also included the fervent hope that Linda would not be typical at all, but exceptional among her peers. She would look carefully and nervously for signs of progress, for success in meeting all the milestones, and for hopeful indications that Linda would be just fine.

But Linda's early progress turned out not to be exceptional. It was more like the kind of progress Lucille could have reasonably expected, which, for an anxious mother wanting the most for her child, felt more like terribly slow progress. She was tireless in her efforts to bring Linda along in those first two or three years, but suffered the frustration of wondering endlessly about why things were taking so long … and what else it was she could be doing about it.

Blending Together

As painfully drawn out as it may have seemed at times to Mom and Dad, Linda's development began to run its due course. The two of them learned quickly to follow *her* schedule. But nothing in what Linda did or did not do would get in the way of life as they planned it or other things required of them. Austin dug in his heels at work. Nothing would be more important to him than being a good provider, and that meant being as skilled and as indispensable as he could make himself at work. In 1952, he embarked on two years of night school to study electricity and auto engine tuning in an effort to enhance his credentials as a machinist. Higher earnings were important, but so was a tighter grip on a good job that had slipped away once before.

Austin and Lucille also imagined a big family, a rich tradition among south-side Catholics as well as a sure way to fill a house with fun, togetherness, and a little bit of healthy competition. Linda, already the beneficiary of a good, helpful brother in Tom, welcomed a second one when Greg was born in March of '53. Her only sister, Cindy, came along in January of '55; and little Steve would round out the Bradley bunch in August of '60. If pure chance decided which of the Lindas of the world got matched up with a good family, then Linda was one of the lucky ones.

25

Dad with (l-r) Linda, Greg, and Tom

Mom with (l-r) Linda, Greg, and Tom

Bumps and bruises commenced as the house filled up with the little ones—five under age 11 by the time the Fabulous '50s were behind them. The kids played well together, but they also squabbled, did a little rough-housing, and every now and then, picked sides to plot diabolical tricks on one another. It's what kids

Playing in the back yard (l-r) Tom, Linda, Cindy, and Greg Bradley

While Mom and Dad relax

did, and Linda was no different. It was a happy home, so they laughed a lot, and they got hurt once in a while. They carried grudges that may have lasted for all of an hour or so before things were back to normal again. They gave each other cooties and then actual germs, sharing their illnesses equally, but they weren't fragile. As the family history has it, Linda alone managed to fight off chicken pox, the mumps, and the measles all in one year.

In the middle of it all stood Mom and Dad playing referee half the time and happy accomplice in the chaos the other half. Mom concentrated on juggling the kids while Dad was the chief disciplinarian. But both knew how to keep things in perspective by finding ways to have a little fun of their own on the side. In April 1958, Austin and Lucille were awarded square dance diplomas, proof enough that they could enjoy a healthy social life alongside parenthood. The ventures from the home front also demonstrated the luxury of good family and friends to pick from when they needed brave, willing babysitters.

It didn't take long for the needs of the Bradley household to outgrow the old rental house on Tabor Street. Austin wasn't afraid to shoehorn a major project into his "spare" time, so he bought a piece of property on the suburban south side where he broke ground on a new family home. He was wise in the ways of construction as well as the realities of what a man could and could not do alone, so he enlisted a couple of friends to help with a few major components. But for all practical purposes, Austin built that house by himself, and his work, beginning on the day in 1958 when he moved his family into the sturdy new limestone ranch at 47 East National Avenue, would prove to be equal to the test of time. It was the Bradley place.

A Place for Linda

Lucille was no less busy in those days. Her children were all under construction, too, and one of the more time-consuming parts of her job involved a search for the proper education for a little girl with Down syndrome. She knew that as Linda reached the age of 5 or 6, she would begin to require the kind of help that even the most energetic moms could not provide at home. Linda would need some level of specialized training and socialization, and Lucille saw it coming since the day they came home from the hospital.

Mom didn't quite know where she would find that, but she kept asking around and she kept looking. In February 1953, when Linda was just 2, Lucille attended a meeting of parents interested in establishing a school for children with developmental disabilities. Like Lucille, these were parents who had declined their doctors' recommendations to send infant sons and daughters off to institutions. They were parents who chose to keep their children, and keep them at home; parents now sharing the isolation and the frustration of having nothing available to help them socialize and educate their little ones. They called themselves "Parents and Friends of Retarded Children."

The group formed a board and drafted a budget, and then began raising funds. Seven months later, they established a new school downtown at 617 East New York Street in an old hall adjacent to St. Joseph Catholic Church. The sign out front described it as "a private school for retarded children supported as a community project," and the board named it the *Noble* School—not just because it was a *noble* endeavor, but because the facility was situated near Noble Street (now College Avenue). The school opened to thirty-one eager disabled students that fall, filling an urgent need for families throughout the city. And many years later, leaders of the Noble School would look back with pride at the significance and the beautiful simplicity of that moment: "For many of the children, it was their first opportunity to dress up, laugh and play, and enjoy cake and ice cream with other children." Linda had gotten lucky again, this time just to be in Indianapolis, where a program like that could get off the ground.

The new Noble School caught on, and its enrollment expanded so quickly that it outgrew the old St. Joseph hall within a few short years. In 1957, with the help of Lilly Endowment of Indianapolis, Noble relocated to the former Orchard School building at 615 West 43rd Street on the north side and then began adding branch locations to improve accessibility to services throughout the city.

Lucille's participation in the cause and her early advocacy for Linda's education helped her witness the city's first generation of sustainable programs for children with developmental disabilities. And the private initiatives that gained steam in the mid-1950s led eventually to mandated public school programs. The early battles on Linda's behalf were far from over, but now, for the first time, the Bradleys had a starting point and an option—just in time for Linda's first day of school.

The first step was having her evaluated to establish a clinical baseline: What was her medical diagnosis? What would she be capable of? In August 1959, the same year in which Dr. Lejeune first identified Down syndrome as a chromosomal condition, Dr. Wesley A. Dunn of the Marion County Child Guidance Clinic presented the first official record of Linda's condition by listing the "nature of her retardation" as "Mongolism." A section of the form requesting the age in months at which Linda was able to achieve certain physical development milestones was left largely blank, which meant no one other than Lucille was keeping track. But the report was less ambiguous in other regards: Linda was up-to-date on her shots, she'd never had any diseases, she was in generally good health, and she was known to get along very well with other children. There wasn't much in the doctor's report to hint at what, specifically, Linda would need in the way of schooling, but the evaluation was good enough to earn her a place in line for enrollment in one of the new special education programs.

Special Education

Three months later, in November 1959, Lucille completed an application for Linda's admission to Noble Schools; a week after that, Linda was accepted and admitted on a temporary basis to its New Hope branch, a facility at 2225 Kentucky Avenue, southwest of downtown Indianapolis. The letter of acceptance specified that after the first of the year, Linda would be transferred to a new Noble branch still under construction at 1125 South Spruce Street, near Fountain Square on the city's near southeast side, just a little closer to home.

So Linda got her first taste of a structured setting outside of the house at age 8. An experience that would have seemed unimaginable just a few years earlier would now keep her from watching

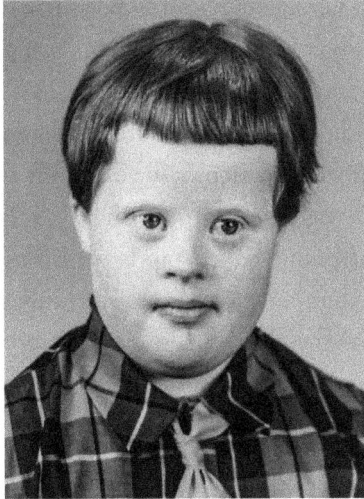

Linda's school photo, New Hope School

The Bradley kids, Christmas 1960

sadly as her brothers left the house for school every morning ... and wondering why she couldn't go too. The new arrangement presented her with an opportunity to develop social skills, to be around other children. But there was some structured learning in it as well, and Lucille had already been hard at work getting her daughter ready. In those relatively quiet moments at home in between the chaos, Lucille and 10-year-old Tom had begun to introduce Linda to the intrigue of letters and numbers. And Linda sat willingly and patiently for every bit of it, tipping her hand to a lifelong eagerness for learning.

The lessons at home helped Linda get off to a good start at school. She loved going there every morning, not just for the social life, but for the chance to show off every new nugget of knowledge she could soak in. Austin and Lucille were in the loop on her progress at school, but nothing was quite as rewarding or official as the first report card coming home in April of 1960. Linda's teacher, Virginia O'Connor, was clearly pleased:

> *Social Progress: Linda has made a rapid adjustment to the group. She is well-liked by the other children and plays nicely.*
>
> *Academic Progress: Linda is handling the reading readiness materials very well. She likes to work with puzzles and is doing a nice job. Her vocabulary is quite large. She handles a pencil well. In working with the letters of her name, she can print "Lin," but is having trouble with the "da." Linda can count to 10 and knows the meaning of one and two.*
>
> *Co-ordination: Linda has very good co-ordination with her hands. She handles her coat and hat easily. She handles her milk and crackers well and can draw a fairly good figure of a person.*
>
> *Conduct: Linda has very nice manners. She is usually well-behaved and is helpful to the other children most of the time.*

Speech: She has a very large vocabulary and good understandable speech.

Linda was off to a good start, and she was right where she needed to be. With the exception of her attendance at a few special programs held at other Noble branches—the 43rd Street location, a new school at the Jaycee Civic Center on Third Street in Beech Grove, and a training center at a Methodist church on South Bluff Road—Linda spent the bulk of her first couple of years of formal education at the Noble School on Spruce Street. Being a good student meant she'd demonstrated a consistent interest in learning and the capacity to achieve most of the objectives set for her jointly by the school and her proud parents. Noble's programs were centered on teaching basic reading, writing, and math skills if those were possible, and helping kids learn to function effectively in a work or social setting. But Linda would eventually need to be evaluated again before longer range learning objectives could be determined.

Public School

In 1961, Linda entered a trial to see which of two learning environments would give her the greatest opportunity to succeed: a vocational course of study or an education in a more academic setting. It was the beginning of an open debate over whether Linda would be classified in the hard, dichotomous language of the day as "trainable" or "educable."

It was a difficult choice in Linda's case because the answer wasn't all that black and white. The evaluators looked at intellectual, physical, and behavioral considerations and saw in Linda strong arguments for placing her in either track. So Austin and Lucille agreed to the idea of taking a longer look; the strategy would keep her at Noble, in a "trainable" class for the balance of 1961, but then transfer her to an "educable" classroom in Perry Township the following year.

Just as planned, Linda closed out the year at Noble in a program focused on vocational training before pivoting to a more academic slant in January of '62, when she was enrolled at Abraham Lincoln Elementary in the Perry Township school system. She made herself at home there quickly, and flourished with enough aplomb to stay well beyond the "trial" period. Linda remained in an academic track at Lincoln for three years, and if the smiles on her face in the annual class photos were any indication, she was more than happy to be there.

Special education at Lincoln helped her improve her reading, spelling, and arithmetic abilities, just as an educable program was supposed to do. And she wasn't shy about giving credit where it was due, repeating frequently a rhyme she'd learned at school: "Mrs. Wright taught me to read and write!" But she may have made her greatest strides from the comfort of her own home, where Mom reinforced what she learned in the classroom. As Linda gained confidence, she began to help Greg and Cindy with *their* homework; she learned by teaching, even if the teaching wasn't always completely on target—or fully welcome.

Things went well, but Lucille wasn't one to hold the status quo if a school or the circumstances changed or if she noticed Linda beginning to need something different. Programs for kids with Down syndrome were new and evolving, so Lucille kept asking questions, and she kept looking for the next best move for Linda. In 1964, Lucille transferred her 13-year-old to a new school in Franklin and then to a different special needs program at Perry East for the 1965-66 school year. She also uncovered social and recreational programs available to Down syndrome kids on evenings and weekends. Every step brought Linda a little further along, and every school introduced something new in her development.

But one thing no school or special needs program could do (yet) was help Lucille with Linda's considerable transportation needs, which meant that Mom was spending a lot of time in the car getting Linda where she needed to go. Dad, of course, was at work during the day and sometimes into the early evening to take advantage of opportunities to work overtime, which meant the Bradley kids, especially the younger ones, were regular, non-optional tag-alongs in Mom's shuttle service.

Juggling Linda's growing schedule with the usual demands of raising four other children wasn't for the faint of heart. Good time management skills were critical. So when Mom could take Linda to programs without bringing the other kids along, she could eliminate the second round trip and be productive between the drop-off and pickup times by taking on part-time work at or near where Linda needed to be. It was usually volunteer work helping out with "the kids" or serving lunches in the cafeteria. Lucille wasn't just an advocate for Linda; she was an advocate for Linda's friends.

Up and Running

Life was normal and busy at the new Bradley ranch in the early 1960s. Mom and Dad had their hands full with work, Dad at the plant and Mom in a house full of kids. Linda was still pretty much attached to her mother's hip, but found a taste of freedom, such as it would be for her, and the joy of her routine as a student. Tom was warming up to high school, Greg and Cindy roamed the halls at St. Roch Grade School, and Steve was an exuberant toddler holding down the fort at

Linda, Greg, Cindy, Tom, and Steve

Mom takes the gang to the park

home. On weekends in the summer, Dad coached the kids'
Little League teams and took the family on camping trips to
Indiana destinations like Brown County State Park and Raccoon

On the front porch at the family ranch

Family photo, 1964

Lake. Families are forever, but they have golden eras—the few short years of the whole gang active and together under one roof. This was theirs.

This was also when Linda's family could begin to see what Linda could be. Austin and Lucille had a head start because they'd been sharply aware for so long of all the benchmarks—the traits and medical conditions linked to kids with Down syndrome and the progress charts used to track their development. They could think back to what the doctor tried to prepare them for and knew, already, there was a lot to be grateful for.

Linda had no major heart defects and showed no signs of epilepsy, leukemia, or respiratory problems. There were, at least for now, no hearing problems or thyroid conditions; and despite the early concerns about the pace of her development, Linda learned to sit, stand, crawl, walk, and talk on a schedule not far behind the norm for high-functioning kids with Down syndrome. Members of her family would answer well-intentioned questions about Linda's progress with a simple, polite reply: "She's just a little slower to do everything." But they were measuring her against all the other kids in the neighborhood.

Early Noble School evaluations of Linda paid particular attention to the manner in which she used her extremities. When Linda was 8, Noble reported "surprisingly good" dexterity in her hands and fingers, and good coordination in her arms, but "Her leg coordination is not as good. She walks with her toes pointed in." A medical examination conducted a few years later by the Marion County Association for Retarded Citizens offered some confirmation in the form of a more complete assessment:

> Linda's upper extremities revealed short stubby fingers with hyper extensible metacarpal phalangeal joints and bilateral simian creases. The lower extremities were equal for range of motion. There was noted to be a congenital absence of the right patella with a forward tilt toward the femur on

the tibia plateau and a rather marked weakness to exten-
sion of the right leg. The right leg was internally rotated.
Her gait revealed a limp to the left and bilateral toeing-in,
worse on the right than on the left.

So Linda did, in fact, exhibit at least one of the familiar profile traits—the deep crease across the center of her palms; and as the evaluation further confirmed, she was double-jointed, pigeon-toed, and born without a right kneecap. None of those things were surprises to her parents, but it put some kinesiology behind what Linda would need to work around. The manifestations of her Down syndrome were a mixed bag that would slow her down, but not much. Even with some of the difficulty she would find in walking—or maybe more accurately *running*—she never thought a thing about any of it. What mattered most, especially to her mom and dad, was that every other measure of her health was described as very good.

What first came to mind to the rest of the world had more to do with the way Linda *looked*. Her features were, of course, consistent with the ones published so indelicately in all the journals: "the small stature, the short neck, the low muscle tone, the slight upward slant in the eyes, and the flat nasal bridge." Linda had at least a little bit of all of those things. But something else about her kept most people from noticing any of it—the bold blend of her bright red hair, the fair skin of her sweet, round face, and a hair-trigger grin that lit up a room.

Linda's trademark smile was always front and center, but she could draw attention for other reasons too. Tom, Greg, Cindy, and Steve grew up alert to the way people reacted to her. To their friends in the neighborhood, she was always just one of the Bradley kids, and they gravitated to her naturally. Linda was an open book, friendly to *everyone*, and while most strangers returned the favor, others, most often other children, could be very different. Some mocked her, probably for no reason other than to entertain their buddies. But that was rare. Others were just a little bit afraid of her, as the Bradleys saw it. In either case, any unpleasant exchanges usually started with someone "looking at her funny."

The "look" was usually the extent of any contention. It irritated Linda's protective siblings, but they knew to ignore it. Insults and name calling, though, were another matter. The kids in the neighborhood knew all the words because they were the same ones used everywhere else—and by the medical profession. The doctor who diagnosed Linda as "Mongoloid" had no apparent reservations about labelling her with a term synonymous with unflattering facial features. It wasn't dropped from acceptable vernacular until the early 1970s, and it wasn't until 2010 that Rosa's Law required the removal of the word "retarded" from federal legislation.

What the Bradley kids would have heard most frequently on the street were society's shorter versions of the unkind terminology, names like "idiot," and "retard." They recalled only a few occurrences escalating into a fight. The Bradleys, the boys in particular, always itched to "make things right," but Mom and Dad's advice on the subject always rang in their ears as they thought about it: "You just can't do that." It also helped that Austin and Lucille made a point of keeping Linda out of settings where scrapes were more likely.

Inside the security of home life, Linda shared a bedroom with Cindy, her junior by a little more than three years. The two of them got along well in close quarters, except for those moments when Linda just couldn't resist the urge to abscond with her sister's stuff. Two of the boys shared a room too, but apparently with slightly less harmonious results. When Austin built new bedroom space in the basement to ease the crowded conditions upstairs, Mom and Dad had differing views on which of the children would move into the new digs. Dad thought Cindy should be the first to have a room of her own, while Mom liked the idea of separating the boys. Mom won out, but never expected perfect harmony.

Like any family, the kids had their share of disagreements. The boys teased their sisters, *both* of them, relentlessly. It was just part of how they amused themselves. Linda tried to tease them back more than Cindy did, but that only added to the torment. But her siblings all understood the importance of including "Big Sis" in most of the things they did for fun, whether it was playing a board game in the living room or roughhousing in the back yard. Linda's temper could get the better of her, and she had her moments of frustration over finding herself on the short end of a competition, but she insisted on being counted as a full participant in whatever they were doing. And when that was over, she was more than happy retreating to her room to entertain herself.

Practical considerations kept Mom and Dad from planning elaborate vacations, but they made a point of scheduling full-family outings at least once or twice a year to round out their together time at home. Longer trips included adventures to Niagara Falls, Washington, DC, and the Dells in Wisconsin. Linda also loved weekend trips in the family camper—the Bee Line—to the great outdoors, where she never shied away from joining in on long hikes, boat rides, campfires, or opportunities to try her hand at a little fishing, as long as Dad handled the bait. But she was just as happy with day trips like the ones they took to Cincinnati to visit the zoo or see the Reds play. And back home, life was full of special occasions, holiday celebrations, and simple family gatherings.

Linda's First Communion   The Bradley Girls

Linda always enjoyed her rightful place in the middle of all of it.

The Bradley heydays of the 1960s, which included Linda's run through public school and special education, wouldn't be complete without her introduction to the Catholic faith. As with other areas of her growth and development, the options were limited. Austin and Lucille's parish was in no position to provide disabled youngsters with formal religious education classes, but Holy Name Church in nearby Beech Grove was set up to consolidate such a program for students on the south side of the city. So that's where Linda went to prepare for the sacraments. In 1962, after completing all the necessary preparations, Linda was invited to attend a special Sunday morning ceremony in her home church to receive her First Holy Communion. Her walk up the aisle to the altar was extra special because it was a procession of one.

But there were no religious education programs available to Linda beyond sacramental preparation, so Lucille, as usual, went to work on finding one. She started by knocking on the door at the parish rectory. Father Jim acknowledged that nothing was available through his church before suggesting a Sunday school program at a Baptist Temple near Garfield Park. It was the next best thing because it was, at least, *something* and because he thought it happened to be a good place to learn basic Christian concepts. Austin wasn't enthused about the idea of Linda attending anything other than Catholic instruction, but Lucille won him over on that one too, which earned her the bonus of one more trip in the car every week to give Linda what she needed.

The Right Fit

Linda's education, outside of those church teachings, and the debate over which track she'd follow continued into the mid-1960s. Austin and Lucille preferred to keep her in an academically oriented program for as long as it would be of benefit to her, but after four years in that setting, Linda's progress began to wane a bit, and the decision was essentially made for them. In the spring of 1966, Linda was "excluded" from Perry Township schools after "it was felt she had received maximum benefit from educable classes for the mentally retarded." Periodic evaluations of Linda's abilities had consistently placed her on the fence between an academic and a vocational path. She had pushed the envelope in proving she was "educable" longer than anyone might have expected, but she had apparently gone as far as her capabilities allowed.

Perry Township's report also hinted at the possibility that Linda's spirited nature may have played a role in their determination. By the age of 15, she was beginning to show the world more of her personality: a sense of independence—also commonly known as a stubborn streak—and a healthy interest in social life. She was assessed as very capable of working well within a group. Her vision and hearing were good; her speech was "pretty good if she goes slowly enough;" and in terms of eating and other personal matters, Linda "does everything for herself." She was considered "very friendly" to the other children, and "in fact, sometimes, too friendly."

At Perry schools, the combination of Linda's slowing academic progress and what they saw as a tendency to be disruptive were beginning to "prevent her from being integrated into other (new) school activities," so counselors recommended she be transitioned to a more vocationally oriented program. Linda wasn't happy about it, and neither was Lucille. And Mom wasn't shy about letting her feelings be known. Her statement in unfailing support of her daughter was part of the report: "Linda is a pleasant and important member of the Bradley household and presents no behavioral problems at home. She has enjoyed her schooling at Perry Township and shed many tears over missing school."

Lucille and Austin understood, more than anyone else, what Linda could do—and what she could not do. They were disappointed because Linda had been very happy right where she was and because it was so hard to leave anything on the table when it came to her highest ambitions. But they also knew, under the circumstances and in light of the recommendations, that it was best to accept the decision and move forward quickly on her behalf. A few weeks later, Lucille called her friends at Noble to see if they would welcome back a familiar student. Noble agreed to enroll Linda in the fall 1966 Home Arts program at its Fountain Square branch, a pivot back to focusing on her life and work skills.

As difficult as it was for Austin and Lucille to know what was best, and available, for Linda, it was harder yet to weigh the impact those decisions would have on their other kids. As a couple, they never considered issues on Linda's behalf without also thinking about Tom, Greg, Cindy, and Steve. And in those difficult days in the mid-'60s, when Linda went through so many changes and the decisions about her future were so complex, it was Tom who Mom was most concerned about. After all, Tom was the older brother with a heart of gold, and a guy like that is always willing to drop whatever he's doing to help a sister like Linda. He understood her in a way no one else could, and he was happy to do whatever it took to protect her. In the way of family dynamics, Lucille seemed to worry that the caring older brother was helping out so much and so naturally that he was missing out on things *he* needed.

But *all* the Bradley kids stood up for Linda. They were happy if she was happy, and no one in the family was very surprised when she landed back on her feet at Noble, happy and ready for whatever was next. She responded well to the big change of scenery and easily flourished among her new schoolmates. This is what B. Jean Orem, home arts teacher at Noble's Fountain Square branch, had to say about Linda in January 1967 after one semester:

> *Entering our group as a new student in September, Linda became oriented quickly due, in part, to her past pleasant school experiences.*
>
> *She gets along well with others and respects and obeys rules of the group. She is able to initiate work and makes strong effort to complete it.*
>
> *Linda reads, recognizes most of the basic one-hundred words and can sound the more difficult ones out. She prints and writes her name, address, telephone number and the names of her family and friends. She counts to one-hundred by rote and with meaning to about fifteen, perhaps more.*
>
> *She is helpful in Home Arts, sets the table, washes and dries dishes, washes tables, chairs, her own desk and the*

*place mats. She takes our linen out of the washer, shakes it
and hangs it on the drier. She also irons.*

*Linda makes good use of leisure time, she is never idle.
She also joins in group games preferring hop-scotch, ball
games and jumping rope. She also introduced touch foot-
ball. She initiates and enjoys these activities in defiance of
rather poor foot coordination and slow movement; which is
natural to her.*

*Linda appears to enjoy her life and is devoted to the
members of her family and friends.*

B.J. Orem
Fountain Square Branch

The journey to school was one of Mom's favorite duties. She
continued her chauffeuring services after the move to Noble, and
her drive to south Spruce Street was always full of excited chatter
from the girl in the passenger seat. Linda had lots of stories to
tell, and she didn't mind telling them more than once; no need
for a car radio, and that's the way Mom wanted it.

Linda's enthusiasm for her new school didn't wear off when
it wasn't as new to her anymore. At the end of the school year,
Mrs. Orem wrote another progress report, doubling down on
her high regard for Linda:

*Linda has acceptable social habits. Her work habits are
also good. She is able to follow verbal directions, initiate
work, and make diligent efforts to complete her work. She
is totally independent in personal care.*

*Linda uses scissors, paint brushes, crayons, and pencils
properly. She is neat and tidy.*

*In home arts she is very capable and does all assigned
tasks well. She helps prepare the food, sets the table, serves
the food, and washes and dries the dishes.*

Linda is an enthusiastic member in group games despite her [physical limitations]. This girl has apparently been well integrated into all phases of her family life and she reflects it.

As parents, Austin and Lucille didn't get much feedback. They were still figuring things out as they went along, but Mrs. Orem's report card on Linda could have easily been theirs too.

PART FOUR

Adult Life
The World around Her

Work Life Begins

The vocational director at Noble took note of Linda's favorable progress reports, but in light of the history of debate over the proper placement for her, requested a new evaluation to make sure Linda was on the right track. The results were consistent with earlier findings. They suggested that, despite a high level of self-sufficiency, Linda's best chance for safety and success in life called for sheltered work and living arrangements.

Noble's evaluation came with a specific recommendation for a vocational path already in place. In 1958, Noble students had gathered to wash and sort rags that would be sold to paint stores and gas stations. It was a fundraiser—Noble's first ever "employment venture." The concept took hold, and two years later Noble began offering sheltered work opportunities on the third floor of a sprawling warehouse complex on East Market Street in downtown Indianapolis, a facility built and once occupied by the historic Cole Motor Car Company.

The students who were part of the original program were young men and women at least 16 years of age who were considered well suited for routine, repetitive warehouse work. Noble's new sheltered workshop (later named Noble Industries) was based on the idea of contracting with manufacturing firms who needed labor and services of that nature. But these companies were also interested in helping the disabled find useful work. On October 9, 1967, a day after her 16th birthday, Linda was transferred to the Noble workshop, where she was assigned to the new GM contract and went to work sorting and packaging small auto parts and performing preassembly procedures on windshield wiper units.

Linda was proud of herself for earning a paycheck. The money was modest, but it was the work that made her happy. It suited her, and she loved being busy. She was good with her hands. She was precise. She was saintly patient with details and steadfast in her determination not to work any faster than she could. And Noble's review of Linda's first two weeks on the job confirmed her qualifications: "Linda has fine motor skills and a much higher aptitude for tasks requiring accuracy than speed," and that's exactly what the customer was looking for. No big hurry on the work; just make sure the kids get it right.

Linda was officially a productive member of the work force, which was about a third of everything she needed. And she already had the other two-thirds covered—some friends to giggle with outside the house and a trip back home every night to enjoy family life. Of course, family life was evolving right along with Linda. Tom was now 18 and headed into the service, considering himself lucky to get sent to Korea instead of Vietnam. Linda had a tough time losing her older brother and best ally to Uncle Sam for two years, but she still had Mom, Dad, Greg, Cindy, and Steve to stand up for her. Tom, on the other hand, was pretty much on his own. But he didn't feel that way nearly as much on the days he got letters from Linda.

Back home, Linda shared a bedroom with Cindy for a little longer, and they continued to get along well. Like her sister, Linda was responsible for a fair share of the family chores; she made her own bed, dried the dishes, and took on special tasks every

Easter, 1970

now and then. But her mom tried not to ask too much of her. Linda's number one responsibility was keeping herself occupied without relying *too* much on the other kids for her entertainment. Play time included board games and an occasional romp in the back yard with the neighborhood kids, but Linda also needed to retreat to her room occasionally for a little solace. She could spend hours noodling through word puzzles or doodling on her writing pads.

Linda's entertainment beyond family life came from whatever Austin and Lucille could find for her. She wasn't a born athlete, but they wanted to make sure she got plenty of exercise. During the heat of the summer, Lucille took her to the swimming pool to help her keep cool, although Linda really preferred staying cool at home or under a big shade tree. Mom knew she'd have much better luck keeping Linda active if she could find activities that included her friends, and she found a godsend in that regard. President John F. Kennedy's noted advocacy for people with disabilities was inspired by his oldest sister, Rosemary, who was diagnosed as mildly retarded. And Rosemary is exactly who another Kennedy sister, Eunice Kennedy Shriver, had in mind when she created Special Olympics in 1968.

It didn't take long for Lucille to get Linda signed up, and it was the beginning of a great tradition: Mom and Dad venturing out with her on Saturdays for the Special Olympic events held at county schools throughout central Indiana. Linda was energized by the competition and some fun with a few new friends, but the big benefit was getting her to participate in a little exercise without all the coaxing. She was open to trying any Olympic event, but seemed to prefer foot races, where her famously short legs and pigeon-toed gait were never a match for her outsized enthusiasm. It didn't matter. Linda looked forward all week to those Saturdays and every new haul of "pretty blue ribbons" from the Kennedy Foundation.

Special Olympics and her work at "the Industries" were good for Linda's confidence, but they also fed her need for a healthy social life. She met her best friend, Jacque Martin, on the plant floor soon after her first day on the job, and the two became inseparable. When Jacque's parents met Linda's parents, they became good friends, too, and arranged play dates for the girls. They also decided it made sense to do some ride sharing as they shuttled the girls back and forth to work and after-hours activities at Noble. Before long, Jacque and Linda were having sleepovers at each other's houses, where they needed no more amusement than the freedom to act silly all night. But they also managed good conversations about what went on at work, spent hours putting crayons to good use, and hugged frequently to remind themselves they were best pals.

Austin and Lucille felt confident that Linda was settled into a good routine and getting the care and attention she needed. But

Linda and Jacque Martin

they also knew that no matter how good things were, there would always be concerns over which they'd have very little control— the natural worries about how Linda was accepted and treated outside the security of her work and home life.

Linda never attended St. Roch, the parish elementary school, because it wasn't in any position to offer a special needs program. But even if it could have accommodated her in some way, either in separate classes or through a "mainstreaming" approach, Austin and Lucille would have likely declined it. As much as they wanted Linda to fit in, they found it unrealistic to think an arrangement like that would be very good for *any* of the students. As they saw it, Linda's classmates would be slower in their progress because of the disabled kids, while Linda would face a steady diet of the kind of uncharitable behavior kids can have in them, something Mom and Dad wanted to prevent if they could. It was a reflection of who they were that they thought carefully about the welfare of *all* of those kids in deciding what was right.

It was no different now that Linda was a working adult. Lucille's twice-a-day round trip to Noble wasn't the most convenient task of the day for a mom with three younger children at home. So when Noble initiated a program in the early '70s encouraging their workers to use public transportation, it would have been tempting for Lucille to take advantage of it, but she and Austin declined. They always trusted Noble to take good care of Linda on the job and valued their recommendations, but putting her on a city bus was a stretch. Too much could go wrong.

As they got older, Tom, Greg, Cindy, and Steve became more aware of the nuance in how kids *and* adults reacted to Linda. She was a trusting soul, but she didn't have any trouble recognizing animosity or ridicule when she saw it or heard it, and those things hurt her. Like Mom and Dad, the kids were intent on doing what they could to protect her from all that without ever making a big deal of it.

Words and name calling continued to be part of it, although, by now, society was at least beginning to recognize the hurtfulness in the language. By 1967, Noble had taken "retarded citizens" out of its name and rebranded itself as Noble Centers. Two years earlier, a delegation from Mongolia sent the World Health Organization an informal request to stop using the terms "Mongol" and "mongoloids" to describe people with Trisomy21, and the WHO subsequently accepted the name "Down syndrome" as the standard terminology. But it has taken a long time for the changes to sink in. It wasn't until 2010 that President Barack Obama signed Rosa's Law, requiring for the first time the removal of the words "mentally retarded" from federal laws. For the practical Bradleys, what people said and how they said it would, in the end, be up to them. It was just the way it was.

Meanwhile, Linda was working hard and beginning to raise a little hell of her own. In 1969, Service Supply Company moved into the old Cole Building and embarked on the perfect business relationship with Noble Industries. Linda was transferred within the building to the new Service Supply contract and promptly got busy sorting, boxing, and bagging nuts and bolts for the "House of a Million Screws." She was good at it, but found it increasingly useless to go to work every day without bringing some fun and personality with her. A routine eight-week evaluation in 1971 included a new wrinkle to prior reviews of her performance at the workshop. "She was reported to be 'quite bossy' with other clients, and became overly excited about her friends on the job, which interfered with her work." Other than that little hiccup, "Linda was considered cooperative and pleasant to work with, and her productivity was above that of the average workshop client." They were getting a bonus. Linda was still getting the job done, but letting a little bit more of herself bubble to the surface.

In 1974, Noble Industries moved its growing employment enterprise to a newly constructed workshop at 2400 North Tibbs Avenue, on the northwest side of the city. Linda moved right along with them; when Noble acquired additional contracts for "nuisance jobs" in the automotive industry, they reassigned her to sort and package electrical components. She was always someone they could turn to—capable, adaptable, and ready for whatever they wanted to throw at her.

The Year Everything Changed

Linda was 23 in the spring of 1975, fully underway in a lifetime every bit as rich and complete as it could have been. Her parents made all of it possible. They brought her home. They gathered the patience and energy it took to understand what she needed, and then found a way to get it for her. They let her be who she was no less than anyone else at home. And they taught her right from wrong and how to prosper in life, just like they did for four other children.

But it was Mom who led the way in blazing the trails for Linda. She asked the questions to which there were no answers yet. She uncovered educational and social life opportunities for her daughter at a time when those things were little more than new ideas. She did the heavy lifting in getting her where she needed to go; and she was the anchor at home blending Linda into family life, even as she juggled everything else that mothers do.

She would never have done it, but it would have been a good time to mark progress. The work was far from done, but Lucille had succeeded beautifully in bringing Linda to this point. She deserved to stop and take a minute to be proud of it. So it was ironic, as it turned out, that it was also her time. Lucille Bradley, just 56, died of leukemia on May 27, 1975.

Lucille Bradley, 1918-1975

It was the year in which the US government passed the Education for All Handicapped Children Act, mandating subsidized education and services for kids with disabilities. It was eventually credited with doubling the life expectancy of people with Down syndrome to 60 years. Lucille didn't live to see it. She didn't see the coming advancements in the care of children and adults with Down syndrome, and she never saw the new programs and educational opportunities on the horizon. Her passing was unfair for those reasons, but it was more unfair because of everything else she didn't see. Linda was just beginning to flourish. Tom had started a family, which included the first of Lucille's grandchildren. And the rest of her kids were nowhere near ready to be without her. Greg was 22; Cindy, 20; and Steve, just 14.

It was also unfair that their father lost his lifelong partner at age 56, and that, after years of being a great father and provider, he would now also have to provide what their mother did. But words like "unfair" never came out of his mouth because what happened was just, well, *life*, and he'd take his lumps like everybody else. Besides, there was work to do outside of the plant. There were young adults, a teen, and Linda to look after, even more closely.

Austin couldn't retire just yet, so he tried to do most of the mom things after work. He picked up on some new domestic skills quickly, admitting he'd never be able to do them as well or as thoroughly as Mom did. But he was industrious enough to put his own practical spin on whatever new chores he needed to do. He also immersed himself in Linda's routine at work and Steve's efforts to adjust to high school. He didn't quite have Mom's touch, but he had a way of getting to the bottom line in what they needed to do and where they needed to be.

He was also glad to have help. Greg and Cindy were both in college, Greg to study business and Cindy to become a nurse. But both lived at home, not on campus, so they could pitch in to help every evening and often during the day; Cindy was the closest thing possible to a stand-in for Mom. Tom, long since back from the service, had gone to work for the gas company and lived five minutes away, which meant he was also available, often on a moment's notice, to help out. Aunt Rita Nolan (Lucille's sister), who was always a big part of the Bradley family, served as a constant source of love and support for all of them. Austin's biggest challenge was keeping a close eye on Linda. It helped that she was independent enough to be left alone at home safely for short periods of time, another testament to her upbringing.

Linda, like the rest of the Bradley kids, struggled quietly to come to terms with losing Mom. There wasn't much they could do outside of making it a point to stay busy, so Dad did his best to make sure they kept their minds on their work and their studies. And in Linda's case, now a young woman capable of so much, that meant full participation in social programs at Noble and an expanded version of her favorite pastimes at home.

A New Normal

Austin wisely followed through as closely as possible with the routines Lucille had set up for Linda. The top of the list included those Saturday trips to places like Terre Haute, Ben Davis, Lawrence Central, and Decatur Central, county schools taking turns hosting Special Olympic events. Linda continued to burn up the track in the 50-yard dash, proudly bringing blue ribbons home for another five years. But sometimes Linda's unbridled spirit had her moving a little too fast, at least in part because she didn't like training at home nearly as much as running in the limelight on Saturdays.

Linda with her Aunt Rita Nolan

Dad began to notice Linda working much harder for slower times. She was overexerting herself, and he worried that she'd get hurt. So he signed her up for something a little less strenuous—a Noble-sponsored bowling league at an alley on West Morris Street. Linda found as much joy in that as she did in her Special Olympics, but without all the demands on her heart and those short, overworked legs. All that really mattered was that she was doing something fun with friends like Jacque Martin, but Linda immediately began replacing all those blue ribbons with shiny bowling trophies. Austin eventually moved her up to the bright lights of the Happy Strikers League at Sport Bowl, where she was a weekly regular for another ten years, all of it spilling into additional bowling entertainment *at home*—the hours of telling people about her great feats in the alleys and the weeks of looking forward to basking in the glow of her annual bowling banquets.

Linda's social agenda also included Noble's Tuesday Night Recreation program, special exercise programs at the center, and monthly dances sponsored by the church groups Lucille had uncovered years earlier. Everything was structured almost exclusively for Down syndrome "kids." Linda always introduced herself to the new ones and, more often than not, connected instantly.

What Linda did at home for fun and entertainment didn't change much as she grew older. She listened to music, watched television, and threw herself into just about anything that would let her be sociable. Noble Centers interviewed her from time to time to talk about her likes and dislikes, both at home and at work, and recorded them in a report referred to as her annual plan. It gave them a road map to her interests and what made her happy, which helped them establish goals for her. Thomas Cain, a planning coordinator at Noble, wrote up Linda's annual report in 1995, when she was a seasoned 43. It sounded a lot like most other reports on Linda:

LIKES:

Linda likes all her jobs at Noble.

She likes to listen to music tapes at home, and she likes to sing to them.

Her favorite groups are the Beatles and the Monkees.

Linda likes to watch shows on TV such as "Family Matters," "Boy Meets Girl," "On Our Own," and "Hang On. It's Mr. Cooper."

She likes to eat snacks while she watches TV.

Linda likes to go shopping with her dad.

Linda said her aunt (Rita) takes her to see movies.

She likes the Pacers, the Indianapolis Indians, and I.U. Sports.

Linda's father takes her bowling every week.

Linda likes to call friends on the telephone.

She likes to dance; she dances at home in her room.

She likes to eat out at Jonathan Byrd's and Gray's Cafeteria.

PERSONAL ATTRIBUTES:

Always nice

Always happy

Sweet

Likes to hug

Loyal worker

Makes friends easily

Follows work rules

Has a positive attitude

Likes everybody

Easy to get along with

If Mr. Cain would have given Linda a little more time to list her likes, she would have also named *The Dukes of Hazzard, Little House on the Prairie,* and reruns of *Bonanza* — Hoss Cartwright ranked right up there with her favorite TV stars. She also enjoyed her Barbie dolls, singing in church, collecting cups, and drawing flowers. And it didn't matter what she doodled; she could spend hours with nothing more than a pen and a pad of paper. All of it sustained her, and it gave her things to share with people, things to talk about.

Her responsibilities at work made her happy too. She continued into the late 1970s with her assignment in the automotive products division, eventually earning $71 every two weeks working with coils and armatures. The coils were her favorite job; she would have done it for free. Noble was pleased with her work too: "Linda seems to have adapted quite well to any special difficulties encountered on her employment routines. She works well in settings that emphasize fine motor skills over gross motor coordination, and her present assignment seems appropriately matched to her strengths and weaknesses."

But Linda was also versatile. Early in 1980, Noble built a 40,000-square-foot commercial wholesale greenhouse adjacent to the workshop on Tibbs Avenue, and they plucked Linda from Industries West to be one of its first twenty-five workers—the original staff at the greenhouse. Under the direction of Tom Piratzky, Noble's new greenhouse manager, Linda went to work mixing soils, planting seeds, weeding plots, and transplanting geraniums. But the greatest use of Linda's green thumb was its part in handling the water can. As Kendall Tilton, plant floor manager, fondly recalled, "She was a 'waterer!'" And what she watered mostly was the nursery's crop of poinsettias. In those days, the new Noble greenhouse was the largest supplier of poinsettias for the City of Indianapolis.

So coils were no longer Linda's favorite job at Noble; plants were. She came home dirty, but she loved every minute of a hard day's work. And Noble helped her take the job seriously. In June, Linda began taking classes in horticulture, and a year later, she was studying mulch gardening and flower arranging. The greenhouse, like so many other work and school programs at Noble, invested in Linda, and it paid off. She would be a productive worker at the greenhouse for fourteen years.

At that point, in 1994, Linda was transferred back to Industries West, which would be her last extended assignment at Noble. She became part of a group charged with processing and packaging nylon filament used in architectural and industrial applications. Then she went back into the old sorting and stuffing business; first on an annual campaign filling plastic bags with props and promotional items for people attending the 500 Festival Parade, and then on a project called Dialogue, where she packaged sample medicines and health pamphlets for cardiac patients.

All of that prepared her for work on the American Baby line, an enterprise providing birth mothers across the country with sealed packets containing samples of baby magazines, diapers, wipes, lotions, and other baby care products. Linda was a "picker;" she filled plastic bags with those items and shrink-wrapped others as part of the fulfillment process. Once again, Linda found herself in the middle of a big job in a busy operation. Mr. Tilton, who was in charge of arranging projects for the workers on the plant floor, estimated that Noble Industries prepared and mailed a million American Baby kits every year for many years.

There wasn't any question about Linda being a good worker and a conscientious employee, but that doesn't mean there weren't a few bumps in the road. Austin took the bad with the good, doing his level best to balance them out.

The physical challenges, of course, had always been a consideration in evaluating Linda's performance on the job. A report dating back to 1978 was typical of the profile on record. "Linda is 4' 9" and has an uneven gait, the result of both feet turning inward as she walked. She has a heart murmur, no kneecap on her right leg, a strong left hand preference, and left eye/right foot dominance. An abdominal exam revealed the patient to be mildly obese." Those things probably necessitated a little extra effort from her at work. They were the source of the aches and pains she suffered, silently for the most part. It's all she knew.

Dr. Foley's exam only underscored Linda's ability to thrive despite all of that; and furthermore, his evaluation of her that day detected no shortage of self-confidence.

Linda was somewhat reserved but she is a very verbal young female who is quite appropriate in her behavior.

She is surprisingly well informed with regard to her environment.

She says she is very good at spelling, and proceeded to spell dog, cat, men, women, Mississippi, stop, go, out, in, exit, and Kentucky.

She was able to write her name, address, city, zip code, and phone number for me; and when shown an old school picture of herself with the date, 1966, on it, she was able to calculate her age at that time as being 16.

She was oriented to all spheres today. She gave me the day, date, and year. Her appearance was appropriate and her affect was appropriate.

The report also confirmed Linda's mastery of a few real-world skills.

Linda was quite open and organized in her statements, and had very good recall of information.

Her speech clarity was very good, although she slurred when she tried to talk too fast. She sounded out words phonetically.

She is a careful, methodical worker, who wants to be accurate. She is quite attentive and highly cooperative.

She is dexterous with her hands, even though she has stubby fingers.

While Linda showed little understanding of double digit numbers, she covered this up with bold attempts at guessing!

Other evaluations of Linda from the same year demonstrated a sense of awareness in her as well as a willingness to share feelings of a more personal nature.

She was quite cheerful for her interview, answering all questions in a cooperative, friendly manner.

She told me that she lives with her father and her brother, Steven, who is 17 years old and attends high school. She also stated that she has two other brothers and one sister. The two older brothers are married and live out of the home. She gave me their ages. Her sister is apparently to be married next week, and Linda is quite excited about the fact that she is going to be in the wedding.

Her manner and content of speech reflected a closeness and mutual concern among family members. She stated tearfully that her mother passed away a few years earlier and still missed her a great deal. She stated she's trying to help her father and younger brother by assuming family chores.

By nature, Austin wasn't keen on Linda talking too much about what went on at home, which is why his kids found humor in picturing the most unrestrained version of Linda going on and on at work about things that happened in the privacy of the Bradley house. But Dad never had anything to hide; he just believed in keeping family business in the family. So while he always made a point of expressing his great appreciation for all the good things Noble did for Linda, he had limits in mind on what they really needed to know and what he wanted them to help her with.

His highest priority, of course, was keeping her healthy, at least in part by helping her manage her weight, which became more of an issue as she aged, and by protecting her from those who would harm her. He and Lucille had always been concerned about strangers, or even coworkers, taking advantage of her trusting nature. The threats could be as simple as someone taking her lunch

**Linda as Maid of Honor
in her sister's wedding**

A familiar spot on Steve's lap

or her lunch money, but the nature of the concerns changed a bit as she grew older and more sociable. Austin and Lucille had worried out loud about Linda being a little "boy crazy."

Now it was a father's puzzle to solve—finding a balance between having Linda's caretakers at work stay in their lanes while also asking them to protect her there. Which programs at Noble or elsewhere would be helpful? And which were examples of somebody just getting into someone else's business for no good reason? Linda participated in weight loss programs and many other helpful classes at work, and she was presented with opportunities to learn advanced skills that would, among other things, allow her to go to a store or ride a bus by herself. Austin didn't have all the answers for what was right, but he was firm in choosing the programs for her that made sense to him and politely saying no to the ones that didn't.

By now, Noble offered a bus service specifically for its clients. Austin knew there would be qualified supervision onboard and that it would be a big help to let someone else get Linda back and forth to work every day, so he got her on the schedule. He felt like he'd done an adequate job teaching her some basic home economics, but figured it couldn't hurt to let her take some individual instruction in cooking, daily living skills training, and classes on handling money. He accepted Noble's recommendation that Linda enroll in self-concept classes, even though he didn't completely buy into the need for it. On the other hand, he was much more confident in his decision to let her take advantage of a continuing adult education program that reinforced the reading, writing, and arithmetic skills she had learned in school years earlier.

If there was a theme in what Dad wanted for her from the outside, it was just to make sure someone was watching her carefully on the job and teaching her any new skills that might nudge her closer to her full potential. Sometimes he shared the options and the decisions with his other children, acknowledging that he wasn't always completely sure he was on the right track. But they knew he was keeping her very much on track, both at home and at work. He kept her active, healthy, and safe wherever she went. And he let her be her happy self.

Linda's guardians at the Industries continued to agree Linda was doing well. Noble instructor and plant floor supervisor Barbara Ireland wrote a work review on her that included hints of the challenges ahead, but she couldn't find much to complain about. "She is a nice person who loves to socialize with peers and staff. She is fully ambulatory, but needs occasional supervision. Linda works best with praise—she becomes easily upset when people say things to her that are not nice." All of which would have made her not that much different from the rest of us.

When Linda was 30, the stone ranch on National Avenue was nowhere near the busy home it once was. It still held a family, but a smaller one. It's where Linda and her father looked out for one another while they continued to go about other business. Austin was near the start of a long retirement from Allison's, but not quite there yet. Linda went on gladly dispatching whatever work Noble could put in front of her. And Dad made sure everyone knew Linda was no trouble. She was helpful, she was good company, and he could leave her at home for an hour or two without worrying about her if he needed to.

He continued to make sure she got out of the house for the social time she needed; and when it was possible, which was almost always, he took her on errands with him. She loved hopping in the car to go on trips with her father, even the very short ones like the ride to church on Sundays. He allowed for occasional departures from his normal route, and from home-cooked meals, to satisfy her powerful craving for fast food. At home, he listened to her talk, sometimes at considerable length, about her day. They did the dishes together, and they watched TV in the basement. Dad established routines at home that were exactly what Linda needed, and together they settled into a language all their own—phrases and verbal cues that guaranteed they would understand each other.

Dad and Linda found their way together just fine, but there was still a lot more to the Bradley family than the two of them. The house was quieter now because, almost like clockwork, Tom, Greg, Cindy, and Steve had all moved out to start families of their own. But none of them went far, and none of them could imagine going more than a few days without returning to the home front to check on things. They kept an eye on what they could do to help Dad—and what they could do to help keep Linda happy. Just showing up would do it.

Outings with Dad

Life at Home

Having so much family available to stop in frequently was as good as it could get, but for the especially sociable Linda, that was only the half of it. She didn't so much lose four siblings when

IU Fan

The very popular Aunt Linda

they moved out as gain four new family homes to go visit, all of them stocked quickly with nieces and nephews:

Tom & Sherry: *Angie, Christine, and Amanda*

Greg & Janet: *Jennifer, Christopher, and Melissa*

Cindy & Rudy: *Cory, Gina, Doug, and John*

Steve & Mary: *Lucy, Julie, Katie, Leah, Patrick, Elizabeth, and Austin*

Linda may have been at her best during the years in which Tom, Greg, Cindy, and Steve were young parents. She was sharp, capable, funny, and independent at exactly the time when she could most fully revel in the excitement and chaos of newborns and young children forming an extended Bradley family. She loved her nieces and nephews, and they grew up loving her back. And it became second nature for them to join their parents, their aunts, and their uncles every now and then in talking about the little things that made Aunt Linda who she was. They were called *The Linda Stories.*

PART FIVE

The Linda Stories
A Telling of the Recollections

Linda Bradley was an achiever. A good look at her path in life—
where she went and what she did—is all it takes to imagine the
spirit and the determination she brought with her to the fight.
What's a little harder to explain is Linda's unique character—her
mix of wit, fire, humor, mischief, love, and innocence. For that,
"You just had to be there," and "You just had to know her." So
a simple retelling of a few recollections will have to do the job.
Linda's life was a success story unto itself. *The Linda Stories* are
about the personality and the color in it.

1. Hugs All Around

Some of the experts say it's stereotypical to think of children or
adults with Down syndrome as being somehow happier or more
loving than anyone else. They would not have found Linda Bradley
very helpful in making their argument. Like all people with Down
syndrome, she had her unhappy moments, but Linda was by nature
a joyful, gentle soul relentlessly free in expressing her affections.

She had two big weapons at her disposal. One was the big,
bright smile with the hair-trigger switch. The other was the
famous Linda Hug, which was just as quick and just as freely
given; it barely mattered whether you happened to be her sister
or, literally, any convenient stranger on the street. She greeted
the greeters at Meijer and Walmart. And then, if she could, she

moved in for a hug, and they rarely failed to open up to her as she approached. They were all in.

The friendly associates at McDonald's, whether they were serving her a Bic Mac or cleaning the next table, were equally welcome objects of her esteem. A smile and a little eye contact was all it took to get Linda to jump up and throw her arms around them as she blurted out, "Oh, I love you!" And while the motivation for doing that may well have included her overwhelming gratitude for the burger, Linda was always all about the simple joy of meeting a new friend.

A man's *best* friend was among them. Steve's family always had big dogs, and Linda loved them all, gently wrapping her arms around their necks whenever the opportunity presented itself. And the dogs made it easy; they could see the hug coming a mile away and couldn't run to her fast enough to get it. So it wasn't uncommon to see Linda, short as she was, looking eyeball to eyeball with a family canine standing on its hind legs as it draped its lanky paws over her shoulders. All the slobber in the world couldn't get in the way of the joy of a big hug.

Linda was a magnet for creatures sensing her kindness. Tom took her to a state park one weekend and stopped at a stable to let her see the riding horses. They got out of the car and made their way to a split rail fence where they could get a closer look, and on the other side of the rail, a big, weary horse ambled over to where they stood. Linda lit up, and with a little help from Tom, she got close enough to throw her arms around the gentle horse's neck as she proclaimed, joyfully, her love for it. After a minute or two, an attendant at the stable walked over to lead the horse away to another part of the corral. It followed along dutifully for a few yards before it stopped suddenly and turned to head back to where Linda was waiting.

Her ease in wrapping her happy arms around a dog or a horse or a complete stranger was just a clue to her capacity for affection *at home*. She never waited for a reason to show it. If she wanted a hug, it didn't matter where you were or what you were doing; she was going to get it. Everyone in Linda's family has a favorite story about her, and every story is unique. But they all include a Linda ever on the lookout for a big, warm hug. It was her calling card.

2. And Other Displays of Affection

Linda always had her trademark hugs ready to go, but she had no trouble finding other ways to express herself if she needed to. Sometimes, if the busy or preoccupied object of her affection was passing by too quickly, she just grabbed a hand and held on for dear life, planting a big smooch on it somewhere if she could. If the angle of her approach was off or if something happened to be in the way, she'd just throw an arm around you from the side or the back. However they unfolded, greetings with Linda were never complete until she was sure she had gotten your attention—and said she loved you. But the big, eager grin was all it took to let you know she was glad to see you.

She was inclined to show love for her young nieces and nephews by chasing them around the house. They all giggled as she shouted out playful threats like "I'll sit on you!" and "I'm gonna give you a big, wet kiss!" She had a clear advantage because she was bigger and stronger, but even 5- and 6-year-olds were a lot quicker. So their entertainment together mixed the fun of a good pursuit with the thrill of escaping Linda's special brand of harmless risk. She was competitive enough to want to catch the kids, but the kids knew Aunt Linda was too gentle to hurt a fly.

The age difference between them didn't matter—she and the kids were kindred spirits.

Slightly older family members couldn't help notice something else about the way Linda expressed her affections—a certain disregard for social correctness. Sometimes she liked to convey her admiration for her sister and her older nieces by way of their physical attributes. If they were wearing shorts, she offered up a friendly, "Ooh-la-la. Nice legs!" If the girls were close enough, she patted them on the back-side as they walked by, adding additional commentary as she deemed necessary. On her more affectionate days, she might call out, "Nice tush!" And on days when she wasn't quite as sure of things, she hooted, "Hey! Look at that rear!"

The men in her life couldn't miss her devil-may-care standards for honoring personal space. When she had big news to share, she needed your undivided attention, and to get it, she needed to tell you the news with her face within a few inches of yours. If you could demonstrate that you understood it to her satisfaction, and that you shared her excitement, she wanted to make a point of rewarding you with one of the aforementioned "big, wet kisses" or by placing her hands firmly on either side of your face, while it was still handy, rubbing your cheeks, and marveling, "Oh, you got such a baby face!"

3. Spilling the Beans

The Catholic Church saw to it that all grade-school students partook of the Blessed Sacrament of Penance. Linda was no exception. She knew the drill, and she could say all the prayers, but that didn't mean she understood the spirit of the exercise. And the part she didn't fully comprehend was the part about mortal and venial transgressions being a strictly private matter between God, through the humanity of the pastor, and the wretched sinner. On confession days, Linda never spent much time sweating her own shortcomings; she was too worried about the possibility her sister and brothers wouldn't be completely forthcoming about *theirs*.

The Bradley kids celebrated the sacrament as a group. That way Mom and Dad could make sure they all *actually* went and Linda could get the supervision she needed. They took turns entering the confessional booth along the side aisle while the rest of the family knelt patiently in the nearby pews, either finalizing lists of their offenses for the pastor's consideration or praying a few *Hail Marys* if the forgiveness had already been dispensed.

But they all had more than their own confessions to worry about; they had Linda's. She didn't need a list of sins when she entered the confessional. She knew them by heart and stated them loudly enough for the whole congregation to hear—very clearly. "Steve threw rocks at the neighbor's cat. Cindy yelled at Mom. Tom ran over a mailbox with the car and didn't tell Dad."

And when Linda was finished, she took her place in the pew, but still had too much on her mind to concentrate on her assigned penance. She watched another brother walk into the confessional and just knew he'd leave something out. "Greg, don't forget to tell him about throwing your homework in the trash!"

Confession at most Catholic churches was a quiet, somber affair. But at St. Roch, you had to laugh a little too.

4. Holiday Spirit

Traditions and festive holidays were huge in Linda's book. There was nothing she enjoyed more than having the whole gang huddled around one of her mom's hearty banquets. Good food and family fun were a pretty good pairing, so it's no wonder Thanksgiving was among her favorites.

Summer holidays were a hit because she enjoyed big picnics and playing outside. She was no fan of firecrackers on the Fourth because they were hard on her ears, but she loved watching fireworks from a distance and waving sparklers to patriotic music. Labor Day offered the special attraction of Dad's company picnics, which meant spending quality social time with other families. She didn't much care for the cold weather setting in after that, so Halloween was a bit of a mixed bag. Like all kids, Linda was all in on a good stash of candy. But in her days of trick-or-treating, and then in her heydays of passing out goodies to the younger set, Linda could do without the more ghoulish get-ups. They scared her.

The church holidays were popular, too, because they gave her a chance to show off her fancy duds. They also meant extra-spirited singing during the service and bonus conversation before and after Mass. Linda especially liked the Easter season for its grand display of purple, her favorite color, and the pure entertainment value it brought to her faith: She was an angel in the art of coloring the eggs, and once they got stashed away, a demon in hunting them down.

But the holiday Linda enjoyed most was Christmas. She loved giving and the thrill of simple surprises, including the ones appearing in her bedroom window every year on Christmas Eve. They were the work of her father, who always mixed a bit of lighthearted teasing into life at home. It was a nice contrast to his more serious fatherly side. Sometimes it was about pranking his boys for the sake of a good life lesson. In Linda's case, it was about pulling one over on her during the season as a way to uncork a little of that joy and wonder in her. But it was good for everybody.

It was a simple thing, really. Linda held onto her excitement over Santa's arrival for a few more years than the other Bradley kids, and Dad was tuned in to helping her enjoy the moment in the most tangible way possible. Every year, he asked his good friend and neighbor Chick Springman to slip into a Santa suit and sneak over to the house to peer into Linda's bedroom. His mission was to tap on the window until Linda noticed him and then slip away into the night.

Dad liked the idea of keeping Santa real for Linda, which also helped him show her the wisdom in being more nice than naughty. But what he enjoyed even more was watching the great spectacle of Linda running frantically through the house yelling, "Hey, Santa's outside!! Santa's outside!!"

5. Learning Her Letters

There wasn't all that much available to help educate kids with Down syndrome in Linda's day, so it was a matter of extraordinary fortune for her that she had a mom who never took no for an answer. Like all the great bulldog advocates of the world, Lucille looked under every rock for resources that would benefit Linda. Honing in on the basics—reading, writing, and arithmetic—she uncovered new special education programs at places like Noble Industries, Lincoln Elementary, and the James E. Roberts School (Indianapolis Public School #97). Mom was grateful for every bit of it, so she never failed to summon the patience and energy it took to get Linda into the car, rain or shine, for the ride to and from wherever school was.

And just in case that wasn't enough, she had a back-up

plan—the *family* plan. Linda never came home with homework, so Lucille made homework for her and then helped her with it. That drew Linda, like a magnet, to the school assignments Greg and Cindy brought home. Every day after school, Linda huddled up with her little brother and sister over mimeographed worksheets. She asked questions, sometimes too many. She replicated everything her brother and her sister did, and sometimes she even tutored them on things she thought they might have missed.

It wasn't long before Linda knew enough to invent her own assignments, filling notebooks with spelling and numbers and impressive penmanship. She was content working at her own pace, she was meticulous, and very much like her mother, she was determined. Linda quickly grew to love reading and writing like a hobby, which meant she wouldn't need anyone to *make* her do it. Her formal education, such as it was, was done by the time she was 13, but she never quit learning or wanting to learn.

Linda's older brother, Tom, entered the US Army in 1968 to serve his country in Korea. He was 19 and like other young servicemen on assignment overseas, had his moments of feeling alone, isolated from life at home and all things familiar. Linda was 17 and now 6,700 miles away. But that's when Tom realized how much his little sister had accomplished.

"When I was in Korea, I got a letter from Linda every week—*every week!* I know it took her at least two or three days to write every one of them. She wrote about things that happened in amazing detail—detail I probably never would have noticed if I was right there in the room; 'Greg had a pop tart for breakfast. Cindy got mad at me for looking in her purse. Steve got in trouble for spilling a Coke on the rug.' I was that far away, and Linda made me feel like I was home. Her letters made my day."

So much for predictions from the doctor who said Linda would never learn to read or write—and that she would drag her family down.

6. "Be Like Linda!"

Linda had no trouble finding things to laugh about. All those episodes of pure silliness with her friends were proof of that. But she had a way of turning serious when it was time to get the job done at work. She was a good worker. It was something her mom and dad taught her, not just by what they said to her every day, but by the examples they set.

Thomas Cain was Linda's supervisor on the plant floor in the automotive division at Noble Industries dating all the way back to its original location on Market Street. He remembered Linda's role at work being a family affair. "Linda's personality was hard to forget. She was the sweetest gal! And her parents were just so friendly, and they always did anything they could to help us at Noble. I remember visiting with them in their home down there on the south side."

The social call was all about discussing how Linda was doing at work—and about her parents asking if there was anything they could do to help. She had been assigned to a new project for Chrysler. In those days the small motors used to power windshield wipers were the same ones used in the early automatic window openers. They were workhorse units that could be remanufactured when they wore out, and the guts of the motor included lots of copper wire that, even then, was too valuable not to salvage. Linda's job was to open up the old motors, unwind the coil from the motor's armature, and then drop the unraveled wire into a bin next to her on the floor.

Linda's dad was not unfamiliar with what it took to do a job like that efficiently, and he knew that the part Linda and her cohorts would find most difficult was wrestling to get a good handle on those squirmy armatures as they pulled the wire out. So he got busy building frames they could use to hold them securely in place on the workbench.

Mr. Cain appreciated the business-like approach as much as the genuine interest in being helpful. It made him see where Linda got it. "Linda could do a lot of jobs in the plant. She learned them very easily. And she never complained about anything! It wasn't unusual for me to have trouble with some of the other workers in the plant, and when I did, I'd catch myself telling them, 'Be like Linda!'"

7. A Head for Numbers

Noble Industries testified to Linda's ability to learn far beyond all those early expectations of her. Excerpts from a progress report in her Continuing Adult Education Program highlighted some of her capabilities, which included a pretty good head for numbers:

Linda writes her name, knows her age and birthdate, and can write her address and phone number. She recognized all numbers up to 100 and demonstrated counting skills to 100 by 1's, 5's and 10's. She knew all the days of the week and all the months of the year in order. She could read a calendar and knew the current day and date.

She demonstrated accurate time telling skills to the half hour and knew some quarter hour times. She knew all the names and values of coins presented and could make almost any amount of change. She could identify all the letters of the alphabet and all functional words presented. She knew 14 of 14 spatial relationships and all colors asked.

Linda's mastery of information was also impressive in the form of her ability to recall sets of seven digits. Aided by sheer repetition and motivated, no doubt, by her need of a telephone for her social life, Linda memorized dozens of phone numbers. She was clearly very bright, but she also demonstrated a functional grasp of practical information. And yet, as the Noble report proceeded to suggest, Linda also had a pretty good head for knowing how to get *around* the numbers if she hadn't quite figured them out. She wasn't above *guessing* if she needed to or doing the math *her* way:

> *Linda attempted her Social Security number ... and she really did come pretty close.*
>
> *Linda had difficulty using quarters to give change for a dollar. So if twenty five cents was owed, she counted and paid back the 75 cents in pennies.*

It's probably worth noting that Linda's evaluator may not have known about her powerful preference for keeping shiny silver coins over the dirty copper ones. Motivation was everything in Linda's education—she knew all the prices for the goodies in the vending machines at work, and she knew that none of them required pennies.

Paper money was one of the things she had a little trouble with. Or maybe not. One day her supervisor called Austin to let him know that Linda had attempted to feed the Coke machine with a $100 bill. No one had any idea where she got it.

8. Compliments

Linda had an amazing capacity for connecting with people she didn't know. That big, friendly smile was always her opener in a conversation with any stranger, but her real secret was seeing, in a heartbeat, something that deserved a compliment. Nothing was simpler or more natural for her than saying, "That's a pretty purse." or "I like your shirt!" In restaurants, Linda made a point of stopping servers to say, "Hey, you're a good cook!" But she always found something, even if she needed to make it a little more personal; women were, more often than not, "sweet," and men were "handsome."

Sometimes Linda's heartfelt compliments were oddly neutral, suggesting the possibility she *wanted* to say something nice, but knew she'd be better served keeping her opinion to herself. "Where'd you get the purse?" "Where'd you get the shirt?" She was too honest to say she liked a shirt if she really didn't. But it was still a compliment and still, to Linda's way of looking at things, a place to start a conversation.

Linda's sister, Cindy, remembered one particular visit to a grocery store with Linda. They were in the checkout line, and there were plenty of people lined up behind them. Something—writing a check, fumbling with coupons, or debating a sale price—complicated the transaction and necessitated the exchange of some additional information across the counter. Cindy was always willing to go through a few extra hoops to get a good deal; Linda was always happy to turn the dealing into a talkfest.

The bargaining part came to an end the second Linda smiled at the clerk and said, "I like your hair!" The woman smiled back and said, "Well, thank you!" And then, taking her cue from the driver's license in Cindy's hand, Linda proceeded to announce morsels of information for the clerk that the document alone could have provided a bit more privately, like Cindy's age and birth date. Linda placed extra emphasis on the *year*. Then she leaned in for more emphasis, better eye contact, and a more complete accounting of her sister's existence—her middle name, her phone number, her address, the names of her children, and if memory served, a bit about the family dog. Cindy and the clerk waited patiently until Linda sounded like she was winding down before finally settling the bill to Cindy's reasonable satisfaction. Linda knew how to join the conversation, no matter what else was going on.

There were also times when Linda's compliments landed in a way she may not have intended. She could get mixed up about advertising and brand names, including the name she read on a sign in front of a local drug store. So, for a long time, when she noticed another woman's fragrance and felt compelled to comment, she would ask, quite cheerfully, "Is that *Low Price* Perfume?"

Linda's free-flowing flattery didn't always come out right, but sometimes it didn't come out right on purpose. She was observant, and her observations could be as colorful as they were true to what she was thinking. In social settings or on evenings out that called for getting gussied up, Linda was likely to address any of the beautiful women in her life as "Miss America." And early the next morning, just out of bed, those women were just as likely to hear her call them "Phyllis Diller."

9. The Telephone

Linda had a preoccupation with the telephone, which made perfect sense. It was her most convenient connection to the social life she craved. Mom and Dad tried to limit her time on the contraption because it tied up the line and because they weren't always sure whose time she was consuming, but it was like trying to keep the squirrels out of the bird food. Linda *needed* to talk, so they picked their battles.

For many years, you could bet it was Jacque Martin on the other end of the line. That's the way it was supposed to be. They were best friends, and together they racked up hours on end giggling and chatting away about nothing in particular. But as time went on, Linda began to burn up more of her phone allotment staying in touch with siblings who had settled into other houses, which, of course, included in-laws and a growing cast of nieces and nephews. By then, her phone was one of those long-corded yellow Slimlines hanging on a wall in the kitchen.

Most of the conversations took place early in the evening, and more often than not, the first words out of Linda's mouth were, "What are *you* doing?" The emphasis on "you" seemed like an acknowledgment that it was already obvious what *she* was doing—calling *you*. There was never much time for an answer, though, because she already had the next question lined up: "What are you guys having for dinner?" And after a proper accounting of the menu, Linda's response was a very predictable "Mmmm, my favorite!" or "Ooh, yummy in the tummy!"

But Linda also liked to talk at some length about what had happened at work that day, slipping her regards for favorite coworkers seamlessly into the middle of irritations over the wrongs perpetrated by her adversaries. She could work herself into a frenzy over those things, but the brother or sister on the other end of the phone call always knew exactly when their father had walked into the kitchen. He was mindful of her "bothering" people for too long, and she, in turn, was inclined to stay on his good side if at all possible. So Linda ended more than a few of those conversations on a dime; "Gotta go. Bye."

But the abrupt end to the phone calls didn't make her forget the details of the conversation. She always remembered, in particular, the answers to her question about the menus, and sometimes she was pretty sure she heard an invitation to supper in there somewhere. "Daddy, Cindy said we should come over for supper tonight." And those were the times when Linda's father regretted rushing her off the phone. It left him with a predicament. Calling back to confirm the invitation would be a little awkward, but failing to show up if the invitation was real would have been rude—and Linda always made sure her father knew how impolite that would have been.

10. Family Vexations

As happy and agreeable as Linda was most of the time, a few things could rub her the wrong way. The little redhead had a matching hair-trigger temper, and when it flared, a judicious way of responding might have been to stay away or say something to calm her down. But the Bradley boys could take the opposite approach, fanning the flames a bit longer for the sake of a good laugh. It just meant they weren't treating her any differently than they did each other.

She could also turn a little rambunctious in those angry moments. When she was 7, Linda climbed on top of an end table in the living room, grabbed the family telephone, stood straight up for the benefit of extra leverage, and heaved it across the room in the general direction of her younger brother, Greg. Unfortunately for Greg, the phone she threw was not the light plastic Slimline that would hang in the kitchen a few years later; it was Bell Telephone's old black workhorse table-top, best known for its anchor-like rotary dial base. Some part of the projectile, either the base or the hand-set, managed to catch some part of Greg's head and produced a welt—and a headache. Greg was sure he was just minding his own business in the living room that day and knew Linda didn't mean to hurt anyone, but she must have thought he had it coming.

Some of Linda's little irritations were predictable. She loved all kids, but didn't care much for them walking into her room uninvited to mess with her stuff. It was a pet peeve tailor-made for her brother Steve's sense of humor. He'd grin as he sat next to her on the living room sofa, picturing the firestorm he was about to unleash. He turned to Angie, Tom and Sherry's little girl, and told her she should go into Aunt Linda's room to play with anything in there she wanted. He couldn't get the words out before breaking into a good laugh over the inevitable—the image of a highly perturbed Linda jumping off the couch, a lot more quickly than she normally would, to track down an eager 3-year-old about to plunder her sanctuary.

But all three brothers enjoyed giving her a hard time, especially when they were teens. None of them could resist, for example, hiding something they knew she'd be looking for or making up a story that would be a surefire bet for getting her riled up. Linda would get furious in a heartbeat, just as they planned it, but then, almost as quickly, she would let Tom and Greg know they were forgiven. Little Steve was another story. For some reason, Linda got *madder* at him and stayed mad at him *longer*.

Even as a 10- or 12-year-old, he had no trouble noticing the unequal treatment, so one day he asked her why that was. And Linda was ready with her answer: "Steve, you're not an adult yet. You have to respect your elders!" Steve thought back to those days and chuckled at the recollection of Linda's explanation, and then he noted that, sure enough, after he turned 18, he couldn't recall Linda ever really getting mad at him again.

11. Funny Eggs

Linda was inclined to forage through the kitchen for snacks when Dad wasn't around, which was, in as much as it was enforceable, against the rules. She especially enjoyed having an egg on the sly, but wasn't allowed to get anywhere near a stove. So no matter how she liked her eggs prepared, she couldn't very well cook her own. Fortunately, however, her father was known to boil a few from time to time, and he kept them in a separate carton in the refrigerator; he had a system. The trouble was, Linda wasn't privy to the system—she couldn't tell the difference between the raw eggs and the boiled ones.

Now, while Linda knew to stay away from the stove, she wasn't shy about venturing into the refrigerator when the coast was clear to take a chance on a fifty-fifty proposition. She'd remove a tasty-looking Grade A, cradle it gently in both hands, walk over to the kitchen table, and crack it apprehensively on the flat Formica surface. On a good morning, she had herself a boiled egg. Jackpot! On less fortunate days, she had herself a liquid mess to clean up and got right to doing whatever she had to do to cover her tracks; her father could not know that an egg was missing, particularly not if she hadn't been lucky enough to actually *eat* it.

A few days later, well after he would have noticed it for the first time, Austin called Linda's attention to something curious in the refrigerator. He put on his serious face, the one he used when he was thinking hard and being a good consumer, and he said, "Linda, do you know anything about these eggs? I think something might be wrong with 'em." Linda blurted a quick no and tried unsuccessfully to change the subject before Dad went on. "Well, I think we're gonna have to start going to a store with better chickens because the eggs I got at Cub's are *empty*, and they got Scotch tape on 'em!"

12. A Healthy Appetite

Linda waged a small battle with the scale as an adult, much of it the result of her physiology working against her—the lifelong challenge of burning calories in a body not very well suited for it. But like most of the rest of us, her biggest fitness challenge was a certain weakness for things that tasted really good.

Even as a youngster, Linda had a healthy appetite, so Austin and Lucille knew they'd have to find a delicate balance: make sure she got enough of what she needed without denying her too much of the things she loved. And that balancing act went on for Dad well beyond the point at which Mom could help him with it. Early on in his days as the single parent bringing Linda along on visits to kids' houses for dinner, he realized the two of them would find plenty of good food wherever they went, and he'd have to juggle his role as her dietitian with his reluctance to let his enforcement of the rules cause a scene. He was very careful not to be a party pooper, but Linda developed a reputation for pushing the envelope.

He managed it all with a sense of humor and a penchant for ribbing her in a way that never felt unkind. Sometimes he replaced the spoon at Linda's table setting with a serving spoon. "You won't need this will you, Lin?" It was his way of reminding her she'd need to pace herself to be polite. But it didn't keep her from loading up on whatever was on the menu. She always glanced a bit apprehensively at her father before holding her plate out for a second helping, usually making a point of letting him know she was practicing the self-restraint he wanted from her: "I'm just going to have a *little* more." He was paying attention, but he never stopped her. When they were guests, he just hoped to nudge her gently into slowing down, often by feigning mild astonishment at her failure to remember one of his guidelines: "I'm a pretty big guy, Linda. You're not going to eat more than *me*, are ya?"

Dessert may have been a plate of brownies or a birthday cake. Invariably, Linda was teased with an offer of the smallest piece, and she invariably responded by expressing her preference for a bigger one. Getting the OK from Dad on a second helping of dessert would be an even harder sell, but she would continue to prefer getting his forgiveness over asking his permission. So when she held out her empty dessert plate, once again glancing over to see if he was watching, she was ready. "I just want a *small* piece this time." And when she noticed her father still not looking away, she added, "But Daddy, I said *please!*"

13. Two Steps Ahead

Linda was always up for matching wits with a niece or nephew at the checkerboard. Her version was a large woven rug that could be spread out at a moment's notice on any open patch of the floor. She grinned and rubbed her hands together in anticipation of the competition before plopping herself down on one side of the rug, crossing her legs into an implausibly compact squat. But she was perfectly comfortable. She could sit in that position for hours.

She didn't always win, but victories immediately wiped away the disappointment of any number of losses. A triumph inspired her. It instantly restored her confidence. It made her get up, at last, from that patient, comfy squat to circle the room, grinning triumphantly as she proclaimed her mighty feat before the gathered fans. And she usually completed the victory lap with a simple, powerfully understated assessment of her prowess: "Hey, I'm pretty good!"

As you would expect, at least a little of Linda's success at checkers may have had something to do with an opponent's motives—it was a lot more fun to see her win than lose. But if you watched carefully, you could see she was perfectly capable of seeing a step or two ahead and planning accordingly. It was a skill she also demonstrated in other areas of her life.

In the days when her father was still getting up early to clock in at Allison's, he taught Linda to get up and get on the bus to Noble Industries by herself. He held her to a firm schedule and a simple set of rules, but sometimes she had trouble getting to the end of the driveway on time.

On one such occasion, Linda overslept badly and missed her ride altogether. So she called her brother Tom, who happened to be off that day, and asked him if he would take her to work. Tom, of course, agreed, and they set out together on a pleasant car ride to the west side. Near the end of the commute, Linda took the light conversation between them in a new direction. She turned to him earnestly and said, "Tom, you sure are a nice brother." Without missing a beat, Tom agreed wholeheartedly before stopping to let her continue. "And, you know, Dad is awful nice too." Another pause fell into place. Linda's nice brother smiled through a sense of anticipation and nodded as she went on. "But, you know, Dad worries too much, and we don't want to give him anything else to worry about, do we? So let's not tell him I missed the bus this morning."

14. Pastimes

As a young adult, Linda's official forms of recreation included her bowling nights and her participation in Special Olympics. But she never had any trouble keeping herself busy in between times.

In the comfort of the indoors, Linda's favorite recreation flowed from her love of learning. Her interest in letters and numbers had people giving her writing tablets and activity books, so on most days you could find her clutching the pens and pencils that brought the blank pages to life. She was perfectly content practicing names and words she had learned, but she was also a creative doodler. Flowers were her specialty. And her rewards for filling up a book or a writing tablet included getting a new one—and seeing her finished pieces stacking up neatly in a corner of the room.

She loved spending time with Candy, the family Pomeranian, who sat still and cocked her head in demonstrated curiosity at whatever Linda wanted to talk about. They were best friends, and her reward for listening so patiently was a warm hug and a free pass for all the face licking she wanted. And when Linda played with members of the family other than the little white ball of fur, her games included classics like Uno, Operation, and Hungry Hungry Hippos.

Music was another avocation. Oh, Linda was no musician, but she loved a good sing-along, joyously joining in on favorite audio cassettes and the theme songs to familiar TV shows. But she was equally uninhibited singing in public, lending her voice fully to hymns at Sunday Mass and the national anthem at Pacer games, all of it in a key probably just a little higher than called for and without the luxury of knowing all the words. People smiled. She was easily forgiven.

In the great outdoors, Linda couldn't wander the neighborhood alone, but found plenty to do in the back yard. She was a master of the Hula-Hoop, but not if the object was to spin it, as tradition held, around one's hips or legs; Linda's forte was whipping it wickedly around her neck. She was also usually up for a pitch 'n' catch with a beach ball if she didn't have to go too far to chase down the misses. But she lit up with every successful catch. Just as with her victories at the checkerboard, those were no occasions for modesty; "Hey, I'm pretty good!"

When Steve was 5 or 6, one of his favorite back yard "toys" was a giant inner tube. He and his friends bounced up and down on the thing, but found it *most* fun when they took a little of the air out and laid it at the bottom of the family slide. The boys took turns sitting on one half of the tube as Linda zoomed down the slide and landed on the other. Every landing launched the boys up in the air and into the grass. She laughed as hard as they did, not just because it was fun watching them get tossed like bean bags, but because she knew the fun couldn't happen without her.

The patio was big enough for Linda to run laps on her deluxe three-wheeler. She could take Candy for rides in the wire basket or ring the little bell on the handlebar to shoo people out of her way. It was simple fun, yes, but her deft control of the bike also boosted her confidence —maybe a little too much. From the back seat of the family sedan, Linda had seen her mother, seated up-front on the passenger side, grab the steering wheel when Dad's hands were occupied momentarily with something else, like a map. So years later when Linda sat up front, she too took the wheel with one hand when she thought her father needed help. Never mind that she wasn't tall enough to see over the dashboard or that it never occurred to her to look up. Dad could only grin at Linda's outsized self-assurance; "Why, thank you!"

15. The Code

In the privacy of their lives together at home, Austin coached Linda on a set of rules that would guide her behavior outside the house. He didn't believe in having too many rules though, and the few he had weren't so much the hard-and-fast kind as they were gentle reminders of what she already knew. They also agreed that the rules would stay between the two of them; no one else needed to know. But if Linda began to stray outside the guidelines, Dad would remind her in the form of his shorthand, and that would be the end of it. It was the code.

Near the top of the list was Austin's insistence that Linda make every effort to mind her own business. She had a sharp curiosity about people and the things she saw in other people's houses. Moreover, she didn't hesitate to get to the bottom of whatever intrigued her. Some of it fell safely into the realm of small talk and social graces; "Hey, where'd you get the pretty candle!?" But Linda was just as comfortable asking about the origins of items she found in the closets.

These were clear violations of the rule against being nosy, and Austin dealt with it by putting on his poker face and asking her, in his efficient way, "Nose trouble?" Linda understood the code perfectly, but always had one or two explanations ready to go. "I was just asking, Daddy!" or "Don't worry. I was gonna put it back!"

Another rule was aimed at Linda's considerable powers of suggestion. She didn't mind coming right out and asking for whatever she wanted, but she was also capable of a more subtle approach. She was good at hinting, although not always so subtly. So Austin instituted the *No Hinting* rule. Linda loved eating out, for example, and her favorite places were popular fast-food restaurants. When Dad had errands to run, he took her with him, and she took her place in the front seat of the car, playing the role of tour guide. She recognized all the landmarks and cheerfully pointed them out. "Oh, look over there—Wendy's!" And then in the same breath, she caught herself in a violation of the rules; "But I'm not asking though!"

When it was possible, Linda's chauffeur rewarded her for the good-faith effort at minding her manners; "OK, Linda. We'll stop for lunch. Where would you like to go?" And then Linda, so excited about eating out, doubled down on her agreeableness. "*You* pick!"

Sometimes things in other people's homes were interesting enough to catch Linda's more covetous side. They were always *little* things, and she generally wrapped her designs on those things in a compliment. "I like your pen. Where did you get it?" or "That's a nice cup. I don't have one like that." She always waited a moment in the hope of hearing the answer she wanted; she was closing the sale. The answer she got, more often than not, was, "Oh, you can just have that, Linda." But when the answer she wanted didn't come, her training kicked in, especially if her father was standing there. "But I wasn't hinting."

Linda was consistent though. She was just as eager to offer hints when she was giving things as when she was trying to get them. She gave her father a handkerchief for Christmas one year. As always, he playfully tried to coax her into telling him what was inside the wrapped gift box before he opened it. And she answered, "It's a secret, Daddy. But you blow your nose with it."

16. Collections

It wasn't hard to find gifts for Linda. Like so many of us, she already had everything she needed and even less use for the kind of things people give because they run out of ideas. But anyone could be a hero just by getting her more of what she already had, like those empty writing tablets that got filled in and stacked so carefully in a corner of her room. And she was an accomplished collector not so much because she saved so many things, but because she *treasured* them.

For the fans who couldn't see Linda without giving her something, it was helpful that nothing she ever treasured cost a king's ransom. She collected things like stickers, key chains, packets of Sweet 'n Low, and pop can tabs for the benefit of the local children's hospital. But most people preferred giving her things that required a little more in the way of effort and pocket change. Linda loved combs, toothbrushes, plastic cups, notebooks, and T-shirts imprinted with anything bright and bold. They were the collectibles she was more likely to get caught hinting for, and those things seemed to come out of the woodwork for her wherever she went.

And yet, the gathering and collecting was only half the fun. For Linda, the entertainment was also very much about keeping her treasures corralled. She loved containers—jars, bags, baskets, little boxes, pouches, purses, and colorful canisters for holding those toothbrushes. She savored the work of slipping her collections carefully in and out of those containers over and over again, all day long. She needed to hold her things in her hands, but never for too long. It was the ownership she loved and the order and neatness of having things in place.

But among her many passing fascinations with things to save and stow away, the most enduring was her stash of ink pens. It was the hobby that came closest to being an obsession. Wherever she went, Linda never failed to spot a pen, whether it was a stray Bic on the kitchen table or a Parker tucked away in a desk drawer. She knew Dad had rules against signaling her desires for a thing she wanted, so she "asked nicely," which usually netted good results. She couldn't get enough.

Eventually, though, something or somebody prompted Linda to betray a curious sense of guilt or embarrassment over her riches. Every time she picked up a new gift pen to add to her stockpile, she felt compelled to look the giver in the eye and deny she was hording them; "I don't collect pens. I just like to write with them."

17. Birthdays

Linda kept a spiral-bound notebook filled with carefully written notes about things that were important to her—people's full names, their addresses, and their birth dates. It was also important to her that she made a note of their exact ages, which is why, for purposes of that notebook, she used a pencil with an eraser. Then, like any good keeper of information, Linda verified her notes at random points throughout the year by asking people the same two questions: "How old are you? When's your birthday?" She asked as if she didn't know, but she needed to be sure.

She was also very thorough with her lists. She didn't limit her entries, for example, to members of the family; she included the skinny on friends, relatives, neighbors, and a cast of her favorite celebrities from the entertainment world. Among so many other collections, Linda collected *information,* and it was another of her great contributions to life at the Bradley house. Before the advent of handheld devices that keep track of such things, the Bradleys had Linda. Anyone in the family needing a heads-up on who needed a birthday card, and when they needed it, could count on her. Just ask, and she'd rattle off the details. No notebook necessary.

But the birth date she needed to remind people of the most was her own, and she had a certain shortcut for getting it out to achieve the urgency it needed; "Hey, I got a birthday comin' up on October 8th!" Everyone knew it was the most exciting time of the year for her because she was as likely to say it in January as she was on October 1.

She was also very diligent about tracking her father's birthday. After Austin had aged well and without much angst to a certain point, it became his annual tradition to tell Linda he was turning 39 on his next big day, no matter how far north of that he may have been. It was his Jack Benny joke. When Linda was younger, she made a point of correcting him on it every year and then making a quick public announcement of his *real* age. People needed to know the truth. A few years later, she began to slip a bit in her impressive mastery of numbers...but not in her sense of arithmetic. Eventually the year came when her playful father announced, as always, that his 39th birthday was coming up, and for the first time, Linda didn't correct him. She held her tongue instead, long enough to think about it some. And then she turned to whoever else was in the room and said, "That's gotta be a lie!"

18. Tall Tales

Linda didn't necessarily know everything there was to know about math, but quick thinking and a certain amount of creativity helped her deal with things that didn't quite add up. She had too much self-confidence to let anyone make her feel bad about her shortcomings, so she held her ground by tuning people out if she needed to, insisting on doing things her way, or making good use of a little bit of ... salesmanship.

A continuing education report on Linda once quoted her as saying her favorite leisure activities were "TV, sports, games, crafts, needlework, reading and recreation at Noble." It was an impressive list, but her father wondered where all the needlework was. He let it go because *most* of the report was true. But then he read about all the chores Linda told them she did at home: "She cleans house, dries dishes, folds clothes, sews buttons and cooks breakfast for her dad." Austin grinned in great admiration of her embellishments before boiling it down to a single question: "Linda, what have you been doing with my breakfast every morning?"

Dad developed his own list of activities for Linda, which included getting a little exercise at home while he got his. He thought his best shot at making it happen was to invest in two stationary bikes—one for Linda's use in her bedroom, and one for his use in the basement. That way, they could ride at the same time—and he wouldn't have to change the settings back and forth.

Linda got on board with the program quickly and began comparing notes with her father on how long and how far they had ridden. In her powerful desire to please him and to keep up, she'd finish workouts by telling him, "I rode five miles today!" But unlike Linda, Dad paid some attention to the odometer on the bikes, and he could see her calculations were off a bit. He never let on because he wasn't going to be a taskmaster over such things and because he preferred to prolong his amusement over her little duplicity.

Noble pitched in on Dad's efforts to keep Linda healthy by introducing her to a program through Weight Watchers. She stuck with it for a few years with mixed results, but from her perspective, there could be no doubt she was losing weight. Her supportive family motivated her with compliments like, "Linda, it looks like you're slimming down a bit," which always brought a big smile to her face. It was all the affirmation she needed, and she never missed an opportunity to share the good news with whoever might have been within earshot.

But Linda knew better. She was still sticking to her story more than a year after her employer first reported that she was "no longer demonstrating any attempt to lose weight." And an update suggested she'd been "fibbing about her weight and what she was eating" for a long time. She had, understandably, ridden the wave of praise for as long as she could, but her little secret was out.

So Linda confessed, and her long overdue confession couldn't help but make you laugh; not just because it sounded so preposterously harsh under the circumstances, but because it was delivered with her usual brutal honesty. All the attention over Linda shedding a few pounds ended the last time anyone ever asked her how things were going at Weight Watchers. She just looked down and mumbled, "I got kicked out."

19. The Stars in Her Eyes

Going to the movies was a rare treat for Linda. It was one of the things Tom, in particular, liked doing with her. But there was a certain amount of risk involved. He had to be mindful of picking films on the G-rated side—the kind that drew audiences less likely to be bothered by noise or distractions. So he knew he was rolling the dice the day he took her to see *Walk the Line*. He knew she'd enjoy it. What he didn't expect was the enthusiastic outburst he heard when the star of the documentary made his first appearance. Linda needed to make sure everyone in the theater saw what she saw; "Hey! That's Johnny Cash!!"

She also had a hard time not telling fellow moviegoers exactly what she thought of the story as it unfolded. Most paying audiences didn't appreciate that very much, so it was a good thing Linda developed an equally keen interest in stories made for the smaller screen, where she could comment and editorialize to her heart's content, whether or not there was anyone else in the room.

She had her clear favorites when it came to television stars. As a teen and for a few years beyond that, she could barely contain her excitement over the drop of names like Barry Williams and Jonathan Taylor Thomas. And in between episodes of *The Brady Bunch* and other sitcoms of the day, she pored over photos and stories about the teen heartthrobs gracing the pages of *Tiger Beat*.

Linda's taste in idols and TV programming changed a little as she grew older. In the late 1970s, she listed *The Andy Griffith Show, Little House on the Prairie,* and *The Beverly Hillbillies* as her favorites. And in the early 1980s, her viewing habits turned sharply to *The Dukes of Hazzard.* While she had no appreciation whatsoever for the General Lee, she laughed long and hard at the buffoonery of one Boss Hogg. But her two real reasons for tuning in were Bo and Luke Duke. When Noble Industries asked Linda to share some of her personal goals, she told them she'd like to meet John Snyder and Tom Wopat in person; "Those guys are handsome!!"

Her heroes were the reason she tuned in, but Linda made no secret of her displeasure with the villains showing up on her TV screen uninvited—meaning before she could change the channel. One of them was Sammy Terry, a local personality hosting horror films on Nightmare Theater. She was terrified by his evil laugh and his ghoulish antics. She was also, surprisingly, no fan of the less ghastly Robin Hood, who scared her with the menace of his bow and arrow.

Most of Linda's TV watching took place in the privacy of her bedroom, but she preferred to be sociable whenever she could, and she could be most sociable when her latest favorite TV show also happened to be her daddy's. So during a certain era on Friday nights at 9 p.m., Linda always joined her father on the couch in the basement for the latest episode of *Dallas*, the prime-time soap opera chronicling a wealthy, feuding Texas family in the oil business.

Linda's unquestioned hero in the show was oil tycoon, J.R. Ewing, played pitch-perfectly by Larry Hagman. Much like Ewing's own *Dallas* family and business rivals, Linda could get a little confused by his conniving ways. But she could see only virtue in him, which became part of the entertainment value for her father. While the glint in Austin's eye betrayed a certain appreciation for Ewing's shady business dealings, Linda spent the hour growing furious over the likes of archrival Cliff Barnes picking on poor old J.R. It was must-see TV at the Bradley estate.

20. Gaming the System

When Steve and Mary's family lived next door, Linda enjoyed the great luxury of having *two* homes and, therefore, her choice of two houses to visit when she got off the bus from work every day. But the rules clearly stated she was to go to *her* house first.

Her dad, now retired, kept a sharp eye out for the bus, both in the morning for the daily pickup and in the afternoon for Linda's return. It was the usual bright yellow school bus, only shorter, and on the side, in black script, it bore the name of its manufacturer; *Bluebird*. Like most people, Linda wasn't always happy about having to get up early to go to work, but it helped her to have a villain to blame—something or someone other than the guy who had to poke and prod her out of bed every morning. The something was the bus.

Linda's father tried to humanize the evil yellow enemy showing up at the door every morning by renaming it. He would call it

Birdie. It's possible he thought it would soften the blow of having to get up, but it was also his good-humored way of teasing her about it. In any event, it didn't help. The only good news was that, more often than not, Linda was in better spirits and on better terms with the bus on the homeward journey.

One afternoon Austin noticed that Linda wasn't home when she should have been. So he called "transportation" to see if Birdie was running behind, and if not, to see if, maybe, Linda had failed to get on the bus. He had plans to take her with him to St. Roch church that evening for a fundraiser, the annual parish spaghetti dinner. He was already behind schedule in heading over there, and being late for anything tended to make him a little nervous.

When Noble assured him that the bus was running on time and that Linda was on it, Austin sat down in his favorite chair to wait for her, and then he did what he usually did in his rare moments of sitting still—he fell asleep. When he woke up a while later, he realized Linda was still not home, so Linda's very punctual father could see he was about to be very late.

He was out of options, so he called next door to see if maybe Steve had seen her. "Oh, yeah, Dad," Steve said, "She came by here a long time ago and told us we were supposed to take her to the church because *you* were running late! So Linda went up there with Mary."

Austin hung up the phone, now angry about looking foolish and being so late for no reason. And then he unraveled the puzzle. Linda would not have forgotten the dinner plans. She probably surveyed the situation the moment she stepped off the bus. She must have seen Steve and Mary out on the driveway and, deciding there wasn't a minute to spare, devised her story for Steve quickly enough to hitch the first ride available.

Linda's father calmed himself down before heading out alone for the parish hall, where he found Linda seated happily in front of a heaping plate of hot spaghetti. The St. Roch dinner, which was always very well attended, was also strictly first come—first served. So Dad handed in his generous fundraiser check, watched Linda devour the last bites of her pile of pasta, helped her into the family sedan, and went home hungry.

21. Coca-Cola

No one ever had to guess what Linda wanted to drink. But they asked anyway, and Linda always answered with an enthusiastic, "I like a Coca-Cola!" Of course, she knew she wasn't always going to get one, especially not with breakfast, lunch, or dinner, when she settled for milk or iced tea instead, but it was worth asking. She usually took the disappointment in stride—probably because she had a backup plan at home, which was another one of those secrets she couldn't quite keep to herself.

Tom often stopped by the house to check in on his sister when Dad was away. On one particular afternoon, he brought his daughter Angie along with him, and they surprised Linda with a pizza. The guests proceeded to the kitchen to forage for soft drinks, but couldn't find any, so Tom told Angie to entertain her aunt while he went to the store for Cokes. But Linda stopped him, excited with the idea of saving the day. "Oh, that's ok. I've got some Cokes already. I'll show you!" Linda went to her room, reached under her bed, and gathered an armload. And there were lots more where they came from. Tom grinned in admiration at the thought of Linda smuggling cans of Coke from her father's pantry, maybe just one or two at a time over a few weeks so he'd never notice. Out of curiosity, and just for the fun of it, Angie asked Linda if her father knew what she had under the bed, and Linda answered, "Dad doesn't need to know all my business."

There was something about the sweet beverage and the bright red logo that Linda couldn't resist. And she wasn't alone. Her little nephew Cory was already busy with his own stash of Coke—dozens of unopened 6-ounce collector edition bottles bearing images of sports heroes and historic sporting events, all placed in matching six-pack cartons displayed neatly on shelves in his mother's basement. Most of it had been bottled a dozen years ago or more. They would be worth millions one day.

Linda was a guest wandering through the house when the collection and its colorful green-and-red packaging caught her eye, but all she cared about was the dark liquid inside. When the coast was clear, she grabbed a bottle opener and helped herself to a couple of the treats tempting her from the lower shelf. It put a small dent in Cory's priceless collection, but Linda's cast iron tummy was apparently no worse for the wear.

And yet, somehow, that didn't mean she wasn't discriminating in her taste for sodas. She would have left those bottles alone if they were anything but Coke Classic. And if Cory's mother had offered her a fresh Diet Coke from the refrigerator, Linda would have made it very clear she didn't want it. "I don't drink Diet Coke. I ain't on a diet!"

22. Spare Change

Linda's hobbies established her reputation as a saver. But she was more than happy to do a little spending too. So she also collected coins—not the collectible kind; the kind that worked well in vending machines.

Lucille, Austin, Mary, and Cindy were all at one time or another in charge of packing the lunches Linda toted to work every day, and the meals were complete with everything she needed, including, more often than not, a snack or favorite dessert. She ate all of it gratefully, but the little extras available in the lunchroom, say a soft drink or bag of chips—things the lunch packers may not have fully endorsed—were a powerful temptation. She was always given pocket change for such things, but it wasn't always enough.

In Linda's world, the shortfall had to come from somewhere, and the somewhere was wherever someone in the family may have left a few coins lying around. Her approach to helping herself to them suggested she knew it was improper, but she let herself consider spare change fair game because it was, well, *spare!*

The petty thievery started with the low-hanging fruit—the nickels, dimes, and quarters left out in plain view. And she quickly discovered that her siblings and their families would not be opposed to letting her keep the money if she got "caught." In fact, for most anyone not called "Dad," the approach went well beyond "looking the other way" and ventured into observing from a distance for the fun of it. Steve and Mary's daughters, Lucy, Julie, Katie, Leah, and Elizabeth, loved her too much not to spoil her, so whenever they heard her say, "That's a pretty purse! Can I look inside?" they happily agreed, fully aware of what came next. After fumbling around in the purse, she would report finding stray coins; she seemed astonished. And after getting a cheerful green light from the girls on keeping what she had found, Linda managed to contort her gratitude into a teaching moment: "You need to take better care of your money!"

When Linda's bad habit grew worse, she began sneaking around at night, especially when she was spending the night in someone else's house. Like others, Greg was amused by her antics and couldn't resist watching—or listening. So on one particular occasion when she was coming to spend the night, he planted change in a chest of drawers in the guest room, where Linda would be sleeping, and planned to listen in on the great treasure hunt.

Sure enough, early that evening, Linda found the coins. No problem. And then she proceeded to rummage methodically through every other piece of furniture in the room in search of spare change. Her brother was well entertained that night, but her adventures kept him up a little longer than he had planned. In the morning, he asked her where she got all the change. Linda said she just found it laying around and reminded him, an accomplished accountant, that he, too, needed to do a better job keeping track of his cash.

A certain sense of humor tends to run in the family, so Steve was equally tickled by Linda's mild kleptomania. But he took a different approach to amusing himself over it. One morning, after she had spent the night at his house, he noticed a pocketful of change missing from the pants he had hanging on the bedpost. That evening he left the same pair of pants on the same bed post and squirted the pockets full of ketchup. An hour later, Linda got herself a handful of it. She wasn't happy. But Steve was. And there was no lecture about the proper handling of spare change.

23. The Dinner Table

Linda regarded home-cooked meals almost as highly as restaurant food, so she was almost as quick to offer her compliments to the chef at home ("You're a good cook!") as she was to the server at Bob Evans. More often than not, her praise came as the food was being served, but before she had a chance to take the first bite, so her kudos to the cook may have been more indicative of her gratitude for having a full plate than, necessarily, the quality of the cuisine.

She knew where her bread was buttered, so a clear sign of appreciation was always in order. "Hey, these green beans are good!" But sometimes Linda's expressions of gratitude only *sounded* like a compliment, leaving the chef with decidedly mixed signals. Somehow, the origin of the groceries made a difference to her; "Where'd you get the potatoes?"

None of that meant Linda was a picky eater. With the notable exceptions of cornbread, cottage cheese, and peanuts, there wasn't much she didn't like or wouldn't try. On one particular Sunday afternoon, Greg and Janet took her to a fine seafood restaurant downtown, where they were surprised to see her pick sushi from a picture on the menu. Linda feasted blissfully without ever knowing what it was—or needing to know.

She was also characteristically organized about her eating technique. Linda wanted the food on her plate arranged in distinctly separate piles, and she disciplined herself to finish one before starting another. She luxuriated in the process. But mealtime was also serious business, the kind of serious that might easily lure a tablemate into distracting her from the task at hand just to watch her reaction. It wasn't hard to draw her wrath at the table; "Can't you see I'm eatin'?!"

A good knife licking was a sure sign she was finished with the main course. By any standard, that was a bad habit, but Linda elevated it to a fine art. She didn't just lick off what was left on the end of the utensil; she inserted the blade, almost all of it, into her mouth and wrapped her lips around it as she pulled it back out. It was both a testament to the gusto she brought to the dinner table and a miracle she never cut herself.

Sometimes, as a meal concluded, she let a belch express her satisfaction. She knew better than that, of course, but remorse wouldn't be necessary if she could get her "'scuse me!" out quickly enough. She further absolved herself by reminding everyone of the perfectly involuntary nature of her little faux pas; "I can't help that!" And then, determined not to miss an opportunity, she surveyed the leftovers on the table. Turkey, meatloaf, ham, tuna noodle casserole—it didn't much matter what it was; Linda had a suggestion; "That'd make a good sandwich for later!"

24. The Trouble with Trousers

Linda had a standard answer for most of the good-natured teasing coming from her sister: "You're a pest." But most of the time, Linda added an adjective to make sure Cindy knew she loved her anyway: "You're a *wonderful* pest!"

Sometimes people looking after other people *need* to be wonderful pests. In Cindy's case, those times included adventures in shopping for Linda's clothing. Finding the right size for her was part of the problem. The other was finding the patience to wait as long as it took for her to try them on. Linda was never in a hurry. There was too much to look at in those fitting rooms and too much to talk about on things that had nothing to do with buying clothes.

Linda was also unpredictably fussy about what she would put on. That didn't help either. Easter was coming, and Cindy thought her sister would look good in a nice, new pair of black slacks. So she took her out shopping, and they trudged through at least half a dozen stores before finding a pair that fit reasonably well. Even then, Cindy knew she'd have to take Linda and the pants to a tailor to have the legs shortened. All the running around came with the usual complications and all the extra conversation with clerks, but Linda was happy. That's what mattered.

Cindy was especially pleased to have the long errand behind her because it ended so well. Linda looked great in her new slacks. But a few days later, as they were getting ready for church on Easter morning, Cindy was surprised, and not happy at all, when she caught her disgruntled sister stuffing the new pants into a trash can; "I can't wear these! I look hideous in black!"

It wasn't the last time the sisters would spar over trousers. Linda liked very much to roll the bottom of her pant legs up well above the socks. Whether it was because she thought it was a fashion statement or because she found it more comfortable was a matter of conjecture. She never said. Cindy, on the other hand, always insisted she roll them back down because "high-water" pants made her look ridiculous. Linda would eventually, and very unhappily, do as she was told, but as soon as the coast was clear, she bent over to roll them back up again.

And so it went, over and over again; Linda rolling up her pant cuffs, and Cindy, herself no slouch in the stubbornness department, ordering her to roll them back down. And when she finally had enough of it, Cindy went to her wild card; "Linda, if you don't keep your pants rolled down where they belong, I am not letting you have a Coke today!"

Linda was beat, and she knew it. There was nothing left to do but leave the pant legs down. But there would be no more of this *wonderful pest* business. She folded her arms in a dramatic huff, shot her sister the old evil eye, and let her have it; "Cindy, you're gonna get yours!"

25. Toilet Paper and Other Obsessions

Linda's pastimes may have revealed some obsessive-compulsive tendencies. Her stashes of things bordered on the definition of hoarding, and she had strong, recurring impulses to check her containers and her purses frequently to make sure the contents hadn't disappeared since the last time she checked.

But her overwhelming need to be neat gave her away. Cindy recalled taking Linda to a Burger King, where the ladies room featured one of those paper towel dispensers that automatically rolls out a new sheet a split second after the previous one is torn off. Linda was still tearing off sheets long after her hands were dry, not because she was being unreasonably thorough, but because she couldn't stand the idea of that last stray towel just hanging there for no good reason. She tore them off as quickly as the machine could spit them out—because she couldn't leave them undone. And on that particular day, she wasn't capable of stopping without an intervention.

She had a similar problem with toilet paper, and not just at Burger King. Linda couldn't resist unrolling something itself so abjectly incapable of resistance, so she unfurled those little tubes freely and often for as long as there was ribbon left. It was a waste of paper, yes, but Linda was very good about putting every bit of it exactly where it would eventually go anyway, which meant that nearly everywhere she went, there was a pretty good chance someone would be dealing with a clogged commode.

To her credit, Linda also believed in leaving everything the way she found it and, in some cases, insisted on improving what she found if what she found was out of order. When Cindy took her to the drug store, a Hook or an Osco in those days, Big Sis made it her business to see to it that things were in place. Neatness counted. Presentation mattered. So as the two sisters made their way slowly but surely through the sundries and the toiletries, it wasn't unusual for Linda to stop dead in her tracks at the sight of a lower shelf of merchandise in disarray, even slight disarray. At that point, Cindy knew there was nothing she or anyone else in the world could do to stop her from plopping down on the spot, in the middle of the floor, to fix it. And there Linda sat, smack dab in Aisle Seven, riveted on the work of straightening out row after row of toothpaste.

26. The New Rules

It's safe to say the rules of social conduct in the workplace have changed over the years. What was once accepted behavior might now be considered inappropriate. That was no less true for Linda and her friends at Noble. But in Linda's case, some of the new rules may have been put in place precisely with her in mind.

Kendel Tilton was a plant coordinator and then a manager at Noble Industries in those days. He never supervised Linda directly, but knew her well, and it didn't take him long to say what he remembered most about her: "Well, she was a hugger! When Linda saw you, her first reaction was always to move in for a big hug. She was just very sweet, really nice. But I think she also had a little mischief in her!"

Kendel laughed at the recollection before elaborating. "Linda had this ongoing preoccupation with Rob McCoy, who was a longtime Noble employee. Rob did the initial testing on our workers, found the best job fit for them, and then he did some of the training. He also got involved in most of the general problem solving on the plant floor, so he would have been around Linda's work areas a lot. Linda had a bit of a crush on Rob, you see, and she wasn't the least bit shy about letting everyone know it. In fact, I think she really enjoyed making him feel uncomfortable about all that public affection, especially around the other instructors!"

The image and the setting had stuck in Kendel's head. "Linda's famous phrase about Rob was always, 'Wow! He's cute!' and she would say it with him standing right there, and then she'd rush in with the big, exuberant hug she was known for. You could see it was innocent and genuine, but a little more unrestrained than it probably should have been!"

As a manager, Kendel kept an eye on the new best practices for changing social behavior in the workplace and how the updated rules might translate to his employees. At Noble, in particular, it would be difficult to regulate signs of affection among people with boundless affection to give. But Kendel and his management team felt it was more important than ever to begin teaching their workers new ways of doing things. It would be difficult to enforce, but if they insisted on hugging people, they would need to hug them in a more restrained manner—and "from the side."

It was a worthwhile effort that must have taken hold for many of the workers at Noble. But it didn't take hold in Linda. It failed miserably. Linda's sister wasn't surprised, nor was she particularly disappointed in the results. In fact, Cindy couldn't help but laugh at what she knew was a dubious expectation. "I'm sorry! I don't care. They can try to make Linda hug people *from the side* all they want, but they are never going to keep that girl from hugging people just exactly the way she wants to hug them!"

27. Unfiltered

Linda liked to keep things simple, and she was at her funny best shooting from the hip. A transcript from an old Noble "Client

Questionnaire" illustrates how she got down to business, whether the news was good or not.

Q: Linda, is there anything you don't like about working for Noble?

Linda: "I love working there."

Q: Are there any employees at Noble you would rather not work with?

Linda: "Yes. Donnette. She sometimes bosses me around."

Q: Who do you think is the best worker in your area?

Linda: "Me."

Austin and Lucille never used swearwords, so she didn't learn it at home, but Linda's language could be a little unvarnished too. Tom remembered dropping by the house one day and stepping into the living room to find his dad sitting on the couch by himself, laughing for no apparent reason. It was a really good laugh, stifled for the sake of keeping it quiet, but the trademark glint in Austin's eye was enough to tell Tom something was up. "What's so funny?"

Austin signaled for him to be still and listen to what was coming out of Linda's bedroom. She was cussing up a storm "under her breath," but the cussing was just loud enough to hear three rooms away. The rant was directed at her father and an earlier conversation he had with her about house rules. Just as Tom sat down to join in on the amusement, he heard Linda say, "I'm tired of that bastard telling me what to do!" That's all it took; Tom broke into a laugh a lot less stifled than his father's. Without saying another word, they sat there together enjoying the salty monologue until Austin finally got up and knocked on Linda's bedroom door. Faking an angry voice, he blurted out, "Hey! Are you talking about me!?" Linda opened the door and said, "Oh, no, Daddy. I love you!"

Sometimes Linda's bluntness could have a passive-aggressive quality. Steve and Mary's children had to be careful not to laugh too hard at the dinner table after one particularly busy workday. Mary set the table with a nice bowl of soup. Linda, ever the fan of a big, hearty meal, took one look at the offerings and dead-panned, "Mary didn't feel like cooking tonight."

Her one-liners, delivered with an uncanny sense of timing, carried a certain unintentional risk of offending people. And sometimes what she wanted to say, or couldn't *keep* from saying, just scared the holy bejesus out of them. Mom and Dad took her to the dentist one day, a new dentist. Linda was quite comfortable in the big chair, but the dentist was a little uneasy because he didn't know what to expect from his first patient with Down syndrome. Linda, on the other hand, did her best to set the doctor at ease, regaling him with one story after another before ending with the one about what she did at a dentist's office a few years earlier. The dentist excused himself suddenly and went to the waiting room to have a word with Linda's parents. "Is she going to bite me?!"

28. The Linda-isms

A lot of Linda's flamboyance came from the odd collection of words and phrases that rolled out of her mouth. Linda had a quick wit and a certain knack for storing little nuggets away until the minute she needed them. They were the *Linda-isms*, the things you could never say again without making everyone in the room think of her—instantly.

For Linda, name calling was never anything other than her way of expressing affection. For the longest time, her favorite pet name for anyone was "turkey," most likely because, in the pop culture of the late '70s, that's what everyone called everyone else. Her favorite name for all the nieces and nephews she chased through the house was either "chicken" or "shorty," odd choices since none of those kids were even remotely afraid of her and all were at least her height by the time they were 10. She liked to call Steve "the runt of the litter" and Cindy "my little sis." She also needed to let everyone know which of the brothers was good at what, so on any given day she'd say, for no particular reason, "Tom is the strong one," "Steve is the smart one," and "Greg is the funny one." Who was what could be different tomorrow.

She loved declaring "bunny ears!" even if she wasn't nearly tall enough to pull it off. She responded to every appearance of a camera with "Kodak moment! Click. Click. Click," and acknowledged every ringing phone with "Avon calling!" And outside the safety and privacy of her bedroom, her harshest expression of a disappointment was "Shucks!"

Linda liked to remind the little ones of her seniority—and her role in their lives; "Did you know I used to hold you when you were a baby?!" She always said it as if a clear memory of it was coming back to her in that moment. If you dropped something, she could say "Dropsy!" before it hit the floor. And she was inclined to notice bellies she may have thought were on the ample side, pointing them out, literally, with a finger poke and the extra attention of a car horn; "Beep!"

Good-faith efforts to entertain her were always welcome, but anything resembling a dance move, well-conceived or not, drew any number of happily rendered expressions of her disapproval: "Oh, you're nuts!," or "Hey, you got ants in the pants!" Jokes or wisecracks had her putting you in your place; "Oh, you're a funny boy!" It was as close as she could come to sarcasm. But she had plenty of silliness of her own. There were never any cats in the house, but every once in a while, when things had been quiet in the room, she let loose with a "Meow!" It was her conscious way of breaking the silence and, maybe, reminding everyone she hadn't gone anywhere.

29. Little Improprieties

The innocence that defined Linda was more than enough to earn her most of the forgiveness she ever needed, but that doesn't mean she didn't create a few embarrassing moments for those responsible for her behavior.

As the curious and uninhibited sort, Linda couldn't help inquiring as to the status of ladies, young and old alike, appearing to carry a little something extra along the midsection. Those people were often friends or relatives, including any number of Dad's nieces. But it didn't really matter to Linda whether she knew them; if she noticed the condition, she'd venture over, pat the woman gently on the belly, and ask, "Hey, you got a baby in there!?" And some of them, as you may have already guessed, certainly did not.

Accidental bodily functions were also part of her innocently improper side. Most people have those, of course, but Linda's exquisite sense of timing could have you wondering if they were accidental at all. Take flatulence, for instance. Cindy had a guest over to the house one day, the newest member of the extended family—and eventually an ex-sister-in-law. The woman dropped a pen on the floor and bent over to pick it up. Linda happened to bend over at the same time to pet the dog, and the exertion had her ripping a big one at exactly the point where the woman's face aligned with Linda's rear end. Welcome to the family.

Another impropriety, one less accidental, started in childhood when she was inclined to stumble into things that belonged to her siblings and make them her own. Mom and Dad put an early end to it, but Linda's little larceny habit came back later in life when there was more at stake. Cindy routinely brought her along on trips to the drugstore, and on one of those trips, she discovered something in Linda's hand as they walked through the parking lot back to the car. It was something she didn't have when she walked in. Cindy was furious and marched her back into the store to return the property to the shelf from which it was removed. Linda knew better. She always did, but on that particular day her understanding of right and wrong was no match for the lure of a bright purple toothbrush holder.

On another occasion Dad and Linda went on a dinner outing to a popular south-side smorgasbord with Dad's sister Margaret, her husband, Maurice, and their daughter Kay as their guests. As dinner was ending, Kay found herself witness to another Linda heist, although it wasn't *really* a heist at all since her meal was paid for and everything on the buffet should have been fair game. Kay got a kick out of what she saw, but never mentioned it to Linda's father, who, she knew, would not have found it nearly as amusing. In any event, before they had all gotten up to leave the restaurant, Linda had asked her father if she could go back to the buffet line one last time for another plate of dessert. Austin told her, "Let's not." So on the way out, walking well behind her father but in front of Kay, Linda lifted an unwrapped piece of chocolate pie and stuffed it into her purse.

Nothing else Linda ever did rose to the level of a drugstore theft or caused any serious public embarrassment, but there were other ways to make her sister feel uneasy, even at home. Linda had reached the age at which Mom needed to sit her down for a limited version of the birds and the bees. A day or two later, Cindy's eyes widened in horror as she walked into a room to find Linda huddled on the floor with her 5-year-old brother, Steve, sharing her newly acquired expertise on the woman's menstrual cycle.

30. The Inexplicable Linda

The funny little idiosyncrasies in Linda usually had an element of reasoning behind them. But as she grew older, some became harder to explain. They had her family wondering, "Where in the world did she come up with that?" The trademark peculiarities were difficult to distinguish from the new ones creeping in, possibly the result of her early onset Alzheimer's. The disease was no less heartbreaking in her than it was in anyone else, but Linda managed to let her confusion and the new oddities seem like little more than an evolution of the older ones. And they ended up producing new catch phrases as unmistakably linked to her as the older Linda-isms.

She continued to have strong ideas about what looked good on her. She had already made it clear that, despite her great fandom of Johnny Cash, she'd never wear black, but grew even more selective in her taste for trousers. When she didn't like the ones someone tried to make her wear, she decided they must not be hers; "Those are *Tom's* pants!" Her prescription eye glasses were a fashion statement, but she found them highly inconvenient. She needed the help seeing, but never put them on unless someone was taking her picture.

Her blind spots in sorting fact from fiction in family matters persisted too. Steve, in his typical mischief, continued to get Linda fired up with false reports on Cindy's latest pregnancy, long after her family was reasonably set. And Linda could still not get past her curious misconception regarding two of Cindy's *actual* children. Cory, her oldest son, was Linda's runaway favorite among the four, while Gina, her daughter, waged a futile, lifelong campaign to win her affections. One day Gina presented Linda with a variety pack of colorful pens, a gift sure to make her very happy. Ten minutes later, in a roomful of people that included Gina but not Cory, Linda held up her new pens and proudly announced, "Hey, look what Cory gave me!"

After the laughing stopped, someone in the room reminded Linda that it was Cindy's daughter, not her son, who gave her the pretty pens. Linda looked a little confused and then insisted, "Cindy doesn't have any daughters!" It was part of a curious difficulty in keeping track of who was who in the family, which eventually included her TV family. She watched reruns of *The Andy Griffith Show* and lit up when she spotted Don Knott's character. "Hey, that's Barney Fife! Barney Fife was named after me!"

Linda also developed a need to find explanations for the moments in life that didn't go particularly well. More to the point, she needed someone to blame for the misfortunes she could not otherwise explain. Barbara Ireland, one of her last supervisors at Noble, was the perfect candidate. The two of them butted heads from time to time at work—mainly because Barbara was doing her job, while Linda was beginning to insist more willfully on doing things *her* way.

She came home some days railing on something Barbara had said or done; rants that amounted to little more than comical snippets of Linda's grumpy side. Mumbling, misplaced anger and a little bit of paranoia were all part of Linda's one-sided bouts with her nemesis. But the boss apparently possessed powers that stretched well beyond her authority at work. Linda had misadventures at home too. One of her notebooks might go missing, for example, or turn up in a room where it didn't belong. She'd stew over the mystery and who might have been responsible for a while, and then grow furious as she figured it out; "It was Barbara!!!"

31. Noble Friendships

"She never met a stranger." That was one of the most common ways of describing Linda Bradley. She also had a little bit of Will Rogers in her; she hardly ever met a person she didn't like. Greg remembered the "funny looks" she got from people who didn't know her. "She never seemed to notice it because her reaction to everyone was to smile and be happy, no matter what." And it would have been rare to have the person she just met not like her back.

Yes, there were those times when she happened to express a keen interest in something belonging to someone else—say, a nice pen—immediately after offering them a flattering compliment. It always drew an appreciative chuckle, but no one ever felt anything contrived about her demonstrations of affection. They were genuine.

Linda had a perfectly natural approach to connecting with people. It was no different at home than it was anywhere else— at church, in the neighborhood, in a supermarket, or at work. And there was no place on earth where she could bounce her personality off other people more exuberantly than she could at Noble. She was at home there, free to mix with a larger captive audience than she could find anywhere else.

The Bradleys could trust she was safe there, too, and free to be who she was among friends, whether they happened to be coworkers or supervisors. It was another world with another set of stories, but Linda brought the cast of characters home with her every night, even if by name only. Her family, including her young nieces and nephews, recognized the names without ever knowing much about the people—people like Kendel Tilton and Thomas Cain, plant floor managers; Brent Higgins and Tom Piratzky, supervisors in the greenhouse; and Barbara Ireland, the instructor and supervisor on the shop floor who served so well and so unknowingly as Linda's workplace nemesis.

There was Rita Davis, Noble's communications director; Colleen Whitaker, safety officer; and Jennifer Evans and John Fikles among a cast of happy co-workers. There was Cary S. George. Linda always included his middle initial when she mentioned him, and she always rambled through his name quickly, so it was a long time before anyone figured out she wasn't *really* sharing work space with Curious George. And then, of course, there was Rob McCoy, Linda's production supervisor and celebrated workplace crush—"He's a fox!"

They were just a few of the many good people doing good work at Noble. Linda sang their praises daily. Sure, there were little feuds to be had now and then, but it was part of what made work and life interesting for her. She picked sides, and there were no gray areas. The heroes were faultless, and the villains evil without exception. On those days, when she got home, what came out of her mouth may not have been accurate, necessarily, but it was honest and colorful.

Linda probably held her tongue at work a little better than she did at home, which is part of the reason she enjoyed a stellar popularity there until the day she retired. But it was her personality and her performance on the job that always mattered most. After nearly forty years of service at Noble, Linda's smiling face and her autograph landed on the February page of the 2005 Arc of Indiana calendar. And even today, a citizenship award in Linda's name is presented monthly to a Noble worker who demonstrates her special work ethic.

32. Aging Reluctantly

While Linda was always very good at remembering birthdays, she eventually began to forget them, and the ones she couldn't remember included her own. So when she asked other people to remind her when *their* birthday was, as she always did, she began to decide that's when hers was too. "Hey, you and me, we're having birthdays together!" But, really, what she couldn't keep track of was time. She wasn't sure what *today* was, which is why she stopped saying, "I got a birthday coming up on October 8th," and replaced it with "It's my birthday today!" It didn't matter where in the calendar year we were. She wasn't taking any chances.

In some ways, time began to stand still for Linda. She had lost track of her father's birthday too—right along with the number she always wanted most to remember, his age. Every year, as her family celebrated his big day, she asked him to remind her how old he was, and, as always, he told her he was 39. Linda continued to look confused by his answer, but stopped trying to do the math. Austin was now safely and without challenge 39 every year. As for Linda, she had continued to be sure of how old she was until she was 53, the point at which she decided, for whatever reason, that she didn't want to get any older either. And from that point forward, she turned 53 safely every year.

She also didn't much appreciate her brothers teasing her about her age. All of them, at one time or another, drew considerable entertainment value from calling attention to the gray hairs blending in with the red ones. It made her furious; "I ain't got gray hairs!"

Linda was resolute in her denials about aging, but went along for the ride, and for a shot at stopping at McDonald's, when her father visited St. Paul Hermitage in Beech Grove. He had an appointment to discuss the possibility of having her live there if the need ever presented itself and to let the sisters at the facility evaluate her needs. In a touch of euphemism, one of the nuns referred to Linda's "golden years," and Linda interrupted her bluntly; "But I ain't in my golden years. *Tom* is."

PART SIX

The Color of Living
Lasting Contributions

Business as Usual—Almost

Linda eased into her golden years with a few diminished skills, but not without her sense of humor, her special way with people, and more of her favorite amusements.

When she was transferred from the Noble Greenhouse to Industries West in 1994, she began a twelve-year run of productive work packaging print and promotional materials for Noble's growing list of employment partners. She soldiered through some physical challenges that prompted a few new restrictions for her in operating machinery and working in temperature extremes. She suffered through her moments of confusion and some difficulty navigating the plant floor. But Linda continued to love her work, and she never complained.

Noble kept a close eye on her, noting that she could still perform her duties efficiently, with the possible exception of spending a little too much time in the bathroom, which was a habit not limited to her employment. Linda was just slow at taking care of business, but it didn't help that she insisted on brushing her teeth on most visits; Linda carried her toothbrush and at least one toothbrush canister from her impressive collection wherever she went.

She remembered to stay interested in learning. She never stopped pestering her father to join Noble's Adventure Club, and when she was 48, she did "surprisingly well" in her first opportunity to use a computer mouse and a "pencil" in a Paintbrush program. Her more forgetful side showed itself most notably when she misplaced her prized blue purse. But coworkers found it within a few days, and when they looked inside for proof it was hers, they found forty-nine pens. Proof enough.

One other slight glitch in Linda's workday, apparently, had to do with her struggle to clock in and out on time. It was no wonder. As she walked to and from the workshop floor, it got harder and harder for her not to stop at every restroom, every vending machine, and every opportunity to chat with her friends along the way. She was ok with not being quite as prompt as she used to be; there were just too many interests competing for her attention.

Linda wasn't about to let her age or physical limitations get in the way of her entertainment off the job either. She was still bowling in the Happy Strikers League well into her mid-forties, which was an accomplishment in itself. She was proud of that stylish baby blue bowling bag with the little black Charger 300 inside; it was stamped with her initials, *LB*. And rolling that thing with both hands and the benefit of gutter covers never made it one bit less fun for her.

Care by Committee

The younger versions of Austin and Lucille Bradley were always busy in the here and now, but not too busy to think about the distant future every once in a while. Like other parents, they tried not to entertain the possibility of outliving their children. But statistics and the realities spelled out by the doctors all those years ago told them they needed to see Linda in a different light. As painfully unnatural as it was, they could reasonably count on being around long enough to give her all the care she'd ever need.

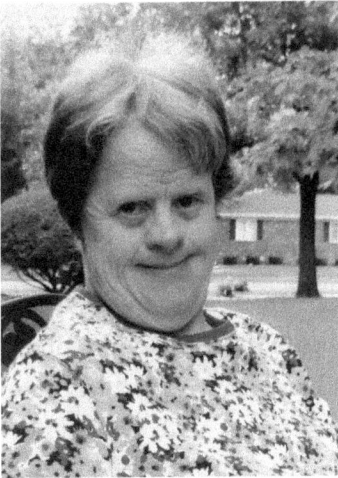

A calm and wiser Linda

Love and a giggle between sisters

But in the same steady way she did everything else, Linda let her parents know she had no intention of falling into the norm; as time went on, Austin and Lucille realized they would have to at least look into what they could set up for her in the event she outlived them. They weren't sure what that would look like, but from the outset, the one thing they knew they *didn't* want was to have any of their other kids inheriting the responsibility for her care on a day-to-day basis. Raising Linda was their decision; they would not leave their children to live with it.

In those days, though, finding "a place for Linda" was a grim prospect, but they listened to the recommendations. At some point in the 1960s, Austin and Lucille visited the Muscatatuck State Developmental Center near Seymour, Indiana, a facility known originally as the Indiana Farm Colony for Feeble Minded Youth and later, in 1937, as an "institution for mentally retarded children." It was a short tour because they saw, very quickly, that they would never let Linda live in a place like that.

The search was still on years later. Austin continued to poke and prod for places that would take good care of his daughter if he couldn't, and he eventually discovered a few possibilities. But while he could see the world outside his house had become more accessible to the disabled than it was forty years earlier, some of those places, even the better ones, would not accept a person with Down syndrome. A representative of one otherwise reputable facility expressed concerns that Linda might make other residents feel "uncomfortable." There were options where there were none before, but it was hard for Austin to think about Linda living anywhere she wasn't completely welcome. So he continued to tell his kids he could handle her needs without help from anyone else—until the doubts began to creep in; "I always thought I would outlive Linda, so I'd be there for her, but I'm not so sure anymore."

When Linda was born, she left the hospital with a life expectancy of twelve to fifteen years. But she was very much alive and well when her mother passed away at age 56 in 1975; Linda was 23. And she was still going strong when her father died at age 85 on July 9, 2004. She was 52.

Her mom and dad made all that possible. They gave Linda everything she ever needed for as long as they could—and then some. But neither of them needed to worry so much about her future. Steve and Mary and the kids moved into the big house next door after Austin passed away, and that meant Linda could stay right where she was and right in her own bedroom, happily surrounded by the love and the youth that would keep her feisty just a little longer. And when she needed a break from the scenery, she had three other familiar homes to visit, all very much ready to welcome Aunt Linda. Despite Mom and Dad's long-held concerns about finding a place for Linda, their other children knew that caring for her

The Bradleys in 2009

was never going to be anything other than a family affair and a community effort. And that's how it turned out.

Carrying On

Tom, Greg, Cindy, and Steve worked together to make sure Big Sis had places to go, people to see, and warm places to lay her head at night. Every now and then for a long time, she asked them the same question: "Where's Daddy?" They answered her honestly, but the only real way to help her was to keep her busy.

She continued her work at Industries West for another two years before being reassigned in 2006 to the Noble Adult Day Services Program, where she helped recycle paper and cardboard, participated in arts-and-craft classes, baked blueberry muffins, and sat for social skills training that included additional, even more futile efforts to get her to hug "the right way."

Linda retired, officially, from her work at Noble in 2007, the proud owner of forty-two years of service. And then, because it kept her busy and made her happy, she stayed on for two more years in the adult day care program before her final discharge in 2009. During that time, she was diagnosed with mild seizures and early dementia, but her emotional health was good, she was still capable of personal care, and she could walk well for a 57-year-old with Down syndrome and bad knees. She was still getting a big kick out of her favorite TV shows, but the one thing she continued to love above all else was spending time with her family.

Linda also never lost that big heart so open to all takers or that smile that lit up a room, but early one morning in 2010, she lost her ability to walk. Linda was taken to the hospital with stroke-like symptoms. The doctors made it clear she'd need help beyond what her families could provide at home, so the Bradleys went in anguished search of the next best thing, and eventually found it in a very hospitable place called the Franklin United Methodist Community.

Linda had no chance of losing her family in the move to Franklin, but it was just like her to find a second one at FUMC. The good people there took care of her as if she *were* family, and in between those caregiver moments in which no patient would be happy, they found joy and humor in her just like everyone else always did. They were quick to make Linda's first family feel at home there too. Her mind was slipping a little bit, but she never failed to light up at the sight of Tom, Greg, Cindy, or Steve and their families stopping by for a visit.

It was a hard few months and yet as good as it could have been. Linda and the spirit inside her made it possible. But it all came to an end when Linda passed away peacefully on December 16, 2010. She was 59. And as always, her family was right there with her.

Linda's family gathers at Buddy Walk, 2011,
in support of the Down syndrome community

Legacies

Linda left the world a better place than she found it. Children
with Down syndrome have a far better chance to thrive today
than they did when Linda was young six decades ago. That doesn't
mean she created revolutionary new programs for the disabled
or lobbied for their rights in Washington. She didn't. But for a
lifetime, she helped people see, one simple exchange at a time,
what a person with Down syndrome is capable of and how they
can add something substantial to the quality of life for everyone.

She held down the fort for a long time while things got better.
Elementary school had been a new idea for a 6-year-old like Linda.
Today there are hundreds of *colleges* with programs specifically for
students with intellectual and developmental disabilities. When
Noble of Indiana was established in 1953, its students and workers
were assembled in one building. In 1996, for the first time, Noble
served more people in community settings than it did on-site.

People with Down syndrome have become increasingly integrated into society, and a deeply rooted perception is shifting; today they are seen not so much as people needing assistance and services as they are people providing them for others.

Linda enriched people's lives with something easily overlooked because it took so little—her easy warmth and the great benefit of a simple smile. That's a contribution she made every day. She was drawn like a magnet to kids. Greg once observed that when his granddaughter Ella was very young, she wasn't one to be affectionate with anyone she didn't see every day. But every time she saw Linda coming, she dropped everything and *ran* to get her hug. That's the effect Linda had on children, even those she didn't know. When the kids brought new friends home, Linda was immediately "Aunt Linda" to them too.

And when Linda made friends, she made them for life. She met Jacque Martin early on in her career at Noble. For a long time, they worked side by side, and they were inseparable after hours. But Jacque eventually moved to a group home, and the two of them lost touch for a while. When they were reunited twenty years later, Linda picked up right where she left off, and the two of them hugged and chatted as if they'd seen each other yesterday. Linda made life better for her friends at work; people who needed company; and other people like her facing similar challenges but without the good fortune of having family nearby.

Some of her friends were friends from a distance. Linda felt a huge hole in her life when her daddy passed away. Greg tried to lift her spirits by hiring a gentleman to paint and decorate her bedroom. Linda talked about everything under the sun as the painter worked, and as usual, she held back no secrets. He listened carefully, but without compromising the quality of his work. And when the job was done, she was so happy and so excited about her bright new room that she sent the man a heartfelt thank-you note. She never saw him again, but when she died six years later, the painter showed up to pay his last respects. And he brought Linda's thank-you note with him. Linda made an impression.

And then there's the matter of family—the Bradley family. It could not have been what it was without Linda. She was the character in the cast offering up so much of the color and the mischief and the humor every family needs, and it was the kind of humor that wore well and without too much sadness after she was gone. Linda's infamous abuse of toilet paper drew out the plunger a little more frequently as she aged. So when the main drain backed up and caused a plumbing nightmare at Cindy's house on the day before her passing, Steve needed only a day or two to laugh and decide it must have been Linda's farewell present for her little sister.

The Bradleys and their children all still enjoy telling a *Linda story* or dropping a casual *Linda-ism* into a conversation. It's almost a language unto itself made up of the inside jokes and the indelible images of her they share. And that, too, is part of what she leaves behind: happy memories that can pop up at pretty much any moment of the day.

But Linda's greatest contribution to the world may have been her ability to bring out the best in people without asking for much in return. She was a contradiction. For someone with special needs, she never really needed anything special. But it would be disingenuous to say she was never a handful or an extra challenge in a busy household. Tom, Greg, Cindy, and Steve all grew up with a good look at what it takes to be good parents, and they saw some of the best examples in how Mom and Dad raised Linda. Lucille was the tireless advocate fighting for everything Linda needed early in life; Austin was the patient soul taking care of her for the next twenty-nine years. All of that rubbed off. None of their other children moved on without the same urge to take care of people—and fight for the underdog.

Linda led a very good life, and she led it with her own flair and her own bold color. She was one of a kind. But earlier in her life, she would have been considered not so much unique as just ... *different*. In those days, it irritated the Bradley kids to no end to see people giving their sister those "funny looks." Steve remembered Mom assuring him that things would eventually be fair and easier; "When Linda gets to heaven, she will look like everyone else." And Cindy gently disagreed; "Yeah, but then she wouldn't be Linda."